CityPack
Madrid

JONATHAN HOLLAND

Jonathan Holland was born in 1961. He moved to Madrid in 1990, having lived for five years in southern Italy. As well as being a fiction writer (his novel The Escape Artist *was published in 1994), he teaches literature at Madrid's Complutense University and is a regular contributor of articles to various magazines.*

City-centre
map continues
on inside back
cover

AA Publishing

Contents

About this book...4

About this book

KEY TO SYMBOLS

✚	map reference on the fold-out map accompanying this book (see below)	🚌	nearest bus route
✉	address	🚢	nearest riverboat or ferry stop
☎	telephone number	♿	facilities for visitors with disabilities
🕐	opening times	💷	admission charge
🍴	restaurant or café on premises or nearby	↔	other nearby places of interest
Ⓜ	nearest Metro (underground) train station	❓	tours, lectures, or special events
🚆	nearest overground train station	➤	indicates the page where you will find a fuller description
		ℹ	tourist infomation

CityPack Madrid is divided into six sections to cover the six most important aspects of your visit to Madrid. It includes:

- The author's view of the city and its people
- Itineraries, walks and excursions
- The top 25 sights to visit – as selected by the author
- Features about different aspects of the city that make it special
- Detailed listings of restaurants, hotels, shops and nightlife
- Practical information

In addition, easy-to-read side panels provide fascinating extra facts and snippets, highlights of places to visit and invaluable practical advice.

CROSS-REFERENCES

To help you make the most of your visit, cross-references, indicated by ➤ , show you where to find additional information about a place or subject.

MAPS

- **The fold-out map** in the wallet at the back of the book is a comprehensive street plan of Madrid. All the map references given in the book refer to this map. For example, the Museo Cerralbo at Calle Ventura Rodríguez 17 has the following information: ✚ C8 indicating the grid square of the map in which the Museo Cerralbo will be found.

- **The city-centre maps** found on the inside front and back covers of the book itself are for quick reference. They show the Top 25 Sights, described on pages 24–48, which are clearly plotted by number (**1** – **25**, not page number) from west to east across the city.

PRICES

Where appropriate, an indication of the cost of an establishment is given by **£** signs: **£££** denotes higher prices, **££** denotes average prices, while **£** denotes lower charges.

MADRID
life

A Personal View

A good centre for excursions

Madrid is divided into twenty-one *barrios*, or districts. Logically, the most central part of the city is the *centro* district. The area of *centro* south of the Puerta del Sol is known as the *barrio popular*, or 'people's quarter', and is a picturesque, atmospheric maze of winding streets. Further south still are the poorer *barrios* of Arganzuela and Moratalaz, which are the result of Madrid's expansion over the last fifty years, and are worth a visit to sample life in the capital off the tourist trail. West from Sol takes you past the Plaza Mayor to the Royal Palace and, beyond that, to the enormous Casa de Campo. To the east of the Paseo del Prado, the Paseo de Recoletos and the Paseo de la Castellana (Madrid's second great reference point after Sol) – a 6km throughway which bisects the city north to south – is the 19th-century *barrio Salamanca*. It is here, and in the Retiro and Chamberí *barrios* just to the south and north-west respectively, that the wealthier *madrileños* make their homes.

When you have got past the clichés – 'wonderfully chaotic', 'energetic', 'all human life is here', 'magisterial', 'from Madrid to Heaven' – Madrid, like all indefinable places, becomes a difficult city to define. At the north end of the city glass skyscrapers rise, hi-tech buildings filled with people working to carry Madrid forward into the 21st century. In the south, away from the tourist trail, abject poverty reigns: shanty towns where wood is burnt for warmth and there is no concrete, only mud. To the west, the Casa de Campo, a huge expanse of occasionally beautiful, occasionally brutal greenery around which the city has had to mould itself; and above, the arching sky, fiercely blue and seemingly so close you could touch it.

History books tell of medieval, Habsburg and Bourbon Madrid, of the transformation of the city into a capital in 1561, of the transformation of that city by Charles III two hundred years later, of the city's heroic resistance at the end of a Civil War which now, for the first time, is beyond the memories of a generation. Artists talk of Velázquez and Goya, and find in their paintings something called 'the Spanish temperament'. The young see the best nightlife in Europe and the worst unemployment, the elderly a city which has changed beyond belief in the twenty years since the death of General Franco. But the day-to-day inhabitants of Madrid themselves are more likely to see their city in terms of the *barrio*, or neighbourhood: be it the wealth of the *barrio Salamanca* or the labyrinthine *barrio popular*, that small triangle just south of Sol where much of the romance of Madrid is still to be found. Here there are picturesque things happening on every corner, and you are continually reminded that you are a fair distance from the rest of Europe.

LOS MADRILEÑOS

There seem to be few *madrileños* who believe in the principle of moderation: they are an extreme people who slavishly obey their current mood. The same person can be friendly one day, and

offhand the next. They are capable of grand passion in the time-honoured Spanish manner, and also of great underhandedness. They believe that it is not what you know, but who you know that counts: numerous government scandals demonstrate this. They are sociable and unreserved: they will ask you where you are from, and when you reply, they will tell you all about it. Their preferred activity is talking – Spain's is a subjective culture, and the word 'I' peppers most of its people's lengthy conversations.

A generation of them still seems a little lost after 35 years of Franco-enforced cultural isolation; the young continue to love their mothers unquestioningly, but they are different now, indiscriminately soaking up Americana. They are moody and proud, though the pride perhaps masks an insecurity about Spain's position in the world, and about Madrid's position in Spain. The majority of Madrid's population comes from families in other parts of Spain, and they lack the strong sense of identity of the Catalans or the Basques. Their *pueblo* – the town from which their family comes – is more important to them than Madrid. Somehow, *los madrileños* retain a little more humanity than we are used to in the late 20th century: they know how to feel, and display, their enjoyment. If Madrid is, as I believe, the most accessible European capital for the visiting foreigner, then it is the *madrileños* who have made it so.

Puerta del Sol, at the heart of the city

Pedro Almodóvar, the *movida madrileña*, and 1990s Madrid

For many young people, film director Pedro Almodóvar represents the spirit of Madrid at the height of the *movida madrileña* – the name given to the period after the political *transición* from dictatorship to democracy. Almodóvar was partly a product of and partly responsible for the *movida*. In the mid-1990s, the *movida* is history, times have changed, and now there are harsh economic realities to be faced. In the 1996 General Election, economist José María Aznar and his centre-right People's Party displaced Felipe González' Socialist Workers' Party, which had been in power since 1981.

7

A Day in the Life of a *Madrileño*

On a working day, the typical *madrileño* rises at about 7:30 after perhaps six hours' sleep. Breakfast will certainly include a strong coffee, and many of the older men like a shot of a liqueur from a bar to set them up. Work begins after 9AM (though earlier in summer when, on account of the heat, offices open at 8AM and close at 3PM). At about 11AM, work stops and it is time for a coffee. Lunchtime is from 1:30–2 until 4:30–5; unless you go to a department store, there are no shops open. This is the time for the main meal of the day. The *siesta* is still maintained, especially in summer, and although there are those who do not agree with it, it is a tradition which will die hard. Shops stay open until about 8PM.

The Spanish evening begins late, and it is not unusual to go out at 10:30 or 11 at night, particularly at weekends. Typically, you will meet with a group of friends, start the evening with a meal between 11PM and 1AM, and then move from bar to bar, having a couple of drinks at each and talking a great deal; the walk between the bars slows down the effects of the alcohol, and it is unusual to see a drunken *madrileño* before about 3:30AM. At this time at weekends and during the summer the bars and discos are throbbing, there are traffic jams and tooting horns, it is hard to find an available taxi, and if you wish to stay up all night that can easily be arranged. At times, *los madrileños* seem almost to defy their bodies' biological needs – but basically, they enjoy the company of other people more than they enjoy sleep.

A passion for football

The Santiago Bernabeu Football Stadium, located north-east of Plaza de Lima on Paseo de la Castellana, is the home of Real Madrid, historically the most successful of Madrid's teams. The stadium holds over 90,000 spectators and is regularly used for cup finals and international matches. For atmosphere, though, the Vicente Calderón – home of Madrid's second team, Atlético – is the better bet.

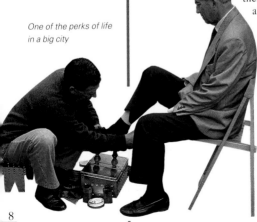

One of the perks of life in a big city

MADRID IN FIGURES

GEOGRAPHY
- Height of city above sea level: 655m
- Average height of Autonomous Region of Madrid: 909m
- Highest point of Autonomous Region of Madrid: 2,430m
- Surface area: 605.8sq km
- Length of Manzanares River: 86km

PEOPLE
- 929: 2,500
- 1202: 3,000
- 1440: 5,000
- 1520: 10,000
- 1561: 17,000
- 1872: 334,000
- 1920: 1,000,000
- 1960: 2,500,000
- 1995: 4,000,000

TRANSPORT
- Number of registered vehicles: 2,000,000
- Total length of Madrid road system: 3,000km
- Total length of metro system: 116km
- Number of underground lines: 10
- Number of No. 13 bus routes: 0

PERCENTAGES
- Percentage of tourists from Great Britain: 3
- Percentage of tourists from Japan: 44
- Percentage of population less than 14 years old: 19
- Percentage of population more than 64 years old: 13
- Percentage of total Spanish population in Madrid in 1860: 3
- Percentage of total Spanish population in Madrid in 1995: 13

FIRSTS
- First gas lighting: 1847
- First railway line (Madrid–Aranjuez): 1851
- First film projection: 1896
- First telephone: 1880s
- First metro line (Sol–Cuatro Caminos): 1919
- First cinema with sound: 1933

A CHRONOLOGY

c 1000 BC	Madrid is inhabited by Iberian tribes.
218 BC–5th century AD	Iberian peninsula under Roman rule; Madrid becomes a stopping place.
AD 711	Muslims defeat Visigoths; areas of Spain under Muslim rule for 800 years.
AD 722	Reconquest begins: Madrid becomes a strategic point of defence for Toledo.
AD 854	Muhammad I of Córdoba founds the city of Madrid.
1085	Madrid recaptured by Alfonso VI: Christians, Jews and Muslims co-inhabit city.
1202	Madrid legally recognised as a city by Alfonso VIII.
1301	Cortes, or Parliament, meets for the first time in Madrid.
15th century	Madrid becomes permanent residence of royalty.
1469	Marriage of Ferdinand and Isabel (Catholic monarchs) unites Aragon and Castile.
1492	Conquest of Granada; discovery of America; expulsion of the Jews; Spain begins 200-year period of imperial power.
1547	Birth of Cervantes.
1561	Philip II (1556–98) establishes Court in Madrid: cultural 'Golden Age' begins.
1598	Philip III (1598–1621) first monarch to be born in Madrid.
1605	Cervantes publishes *Don Quixote*.
1617–19	Plaza Mayor built.
1665	Charles II comes to throne, aged 4.

1700	Charles II dies heirless: Philip V (1700–46) comes to throne as first of Bourbon monarchs.
1759	Under Charles III massive modernisation programme begins.
1808	French occupation.
1812	Madrid's 'Year of Hunger'.
1819	Prado Museum opened; houses numbered and streets named.
1851	Madrid–Aranjuez railway line inaugurated.
1858	Water brought to Madrid via Isabel II Canal.
1868	Revolution overthrows Isabel II.
1873	Republic declared.
1917	General Strike throughout Spain.
1919	First metro line.
1923	Primo de Rivera establishes military dictatorship.
1931	Second Republic declared.
1936–9	Spanish Civil War, sparked off by uprising in North Africa.
1975	General Franco dies.
1977	First democratic General Election.
1980s	'*Movida* Madrid'.
1982	Socialist government elected.
1986	Spain joins EEC (EU).
1992	Olympic games in Barcelona; Expo '92 in Seville; Madrid is European Capital of Culture.

PEOPLE & EVENTS FROM HISTORY

Cervantes, something of a romantic hero himself

Metro stations and the famous

Many of Madrid's streets and metro stations are named after historical figures who are completely unknown outside Spain. Among the central stations, there are Tirso de Molina and Quevedo (both Golden Age writers), La Latina (the nickname of Beatriz Galindo, Queen Isabella II's Latin teacher), Rubén Darío (19th-century Nicaraguan poet), Diego de Léon (army general executed for trying to kidnap Isabella II in 1841) and Chueca (Federico Chueca, a composer of *zarzuelas*, or operettas). Most curious of all is Antón Martín, a 16th-century Valencian coastguard who converted to Christianity after a vision of John the Baptist and then founded the hospital in Madrid. Better known are Colón (Christopher Columbus), Goya and Velázquez. It is a little-known fact that Madrid has a street named after John Lennon.

CHARLES III

Charles III, the second Bourbon king of Spain, came to the throne in 1759. A keen proponent of Enlightenment ideals, he is often known as 'the best mayor that Madrid ever had'. More than any other single historical figure, he is responsible for the city we see today.

MIGUEL DE CERVANTES SAAVEDRA (CERVANTES)

The author of *Don Quixote*: believed by some to be the first novel and by others simply the greatest book ever written, it was published in two parts in 1605 and 1615. Born in Alcalá de Henares, Cervantes fought in the Battle of Lepanto. In 1575 he was taken prisoner by Algerian pirates. Later he became a tax collector, but was imprisoned for fiddling the accounts. It was during this time that Cervantes wrote *Don Quixote*. He died in Madrid in 1616.

GOYA

Francisco de Goya y Lucientes (1746–1848) is the painter most readily associated with Madrid, though he was neither born nor died here. Born in Aragón, he settled in Madrid in 1774 and worked at the Royal Tapestry Factory. It was not until 1789 that he became Court painter to Charles IV. In 1792, Goya contracted an illness which left him practically deaf, and it is to the silence and solitude of his convalesence that we owe the sometimes nightmarish visions of his *Caprichos*. In 1814 he bought a house, the Quinta del Sordo, and covered the walls with the 'dark paintings' now on display in the Prado Museum.

JUAN GRIS

Painter Juan Gris (José Victoriano González), one of the great Madrid artistic exiles, was born in 1887 at Calle Tetuán 20. He began his artistic life as a cartoonist. From 1910 he dedicated himself exclusively to painting and between 1910 and 1914 produced many of the works which make him the greatest exponent of Cubism after Picasso himself. He died in 1927.

MADRID
*how to organise
your time*

ITINERARIES

From a walking point of view, Madrid is not forbiddingly large, though it is best to concentrate on one area at a time to keep a sense of historical perspective.

ITINERARY ONE	MEDIEVAL TO HABSBURG MADRID
Breakfast	A café in the Plaza Mayor (►33)
Morning	Stroll through medieval Madrid (►18) to the Plaza de la Villa (► 32) San Pedro el Viejo (►55) San Andrés (►54) Plaza de la Paja (►53) Plaza de la Villa (►32)
Lunch	Casa Ciriaco (►63) in the Calle Mayor (►59), or back to the Plaza Mayor to the Hogar Gallego (►65)
Afternoon	San Nicolás de los Servitas (►55) Monasterio de la Encarnación (►31) Convento de las Descalzas Reales (►34)
ITINERARY TWO	BOURBON MADRID
Breakfast	At one of the bars in the Plaza de Santa Ana(►53)
Morning	Plaza de Santa Ana (►53) Museo del Prado (►41) Casón del Buen Retiro (►50) San Jerónimo el Real (►42) Plaza de la Lealtad (►53)
Lunch	Viridiana (►62) or in the café of the Prado
Afternoon	Colección Thyssen-Bornemisza (►37) or Reina Sofía (►38) Parque del Retiro (►46) Puerta de Alcalá(►45) Plaza de la Cibeles (►40) Fuente de Neptuno (►56)
Early evening	Drink at one of the *terraza* bars on the 'Costa Castellana' (►79)

ITINERARY THREE	**NORTH-WESTERN MADRID**
Breakfast	Café de Oriente (►68) in Plaza de Oriente (►30)
Morning	Arab Wall (►60) Jardines de las Vistillas (►57) Catedral Nuestra Señora de la Almudena (►28) Palacio Real (►29)
Lunch	El Buey (►63)
Afternoon	Museo Cerralbo (►27) Plaza de España (►52) Ermita de San Antonio (►24) Stroll through Parque del Oeste (►25) via La Rosaleda (►25) to the *teleférico* (►57) Casa de Campo (►57), and then back via the *teleférico* to the Parque del Oeste
Early evening	Templo de Debod (►25), and a drink at one of the *terraza* bars on the Paseo de Pintor Rosales (►79)
ITINERARY FOUR	**NORTH-EAST FROM SOL**
Breakfast	Chocolatería San Ginés (►68)
Morning	Calle de Arenal (►59) Puerta del Sol (►35) Real Académia de Bellas Artes de San Fernando, Calcografía Nacional (►36) Jardines del Descubrimiento (►44) Palacio de Bibliotecas y Museos (►43) Shop in Calle de Serrano (►72) and Calle José Ortega y Gasset (►72)
Lunch	Teatriz (►82)
Afternoon *Window shopping in* *Calle de Serrano*	Metro to Rubén Darío. Museo Sorolla (►39), then Museo Lázaro Galdiano (►47)

15

WALKS

THE SIGHTS

INFORMATION

Distance 6km
Time 3–4 hours
Start point Puerta del Sol
⊞ cII, D9
🚇 Sol (lines 1, 2, 3)
🚌 3, 5, 15, 20, 51, 52, 150 and others
End point Puerta del Sol

Opposite: the Royal Palace, from Campo del Moro

EAST FROM SOL

Start in the Puerta del Sol. Exit at its eastern end and walk down Calle San Jerónimo, through the Plaza de las Cortes, as far as the Neptune fountain in the Plaza de Canovas de Castillo. Turn right down the Paseo del Prado, cross it half-way down, and visit the Botanical Gardens. Cross the plaza and walk up Calle de Felipe IV past the Royal Language Academy on your left, and the Casón del Buen Retiro. Cross Calle de Alfonso XII and enter the Retiro Park through the Felipe IV gate, and walk through the parterre gardens. Go up the steps at the end of the gardens. When you reach the lake, turn left and follow the edge of it, with the Alfonso XII statue opposite you.

Exit the park at the Puerta de Alcalá and walk up Calle Serrano past the Archaeological Museum. Cut through the Jardines del Descubrimiento and then turn left down the Paseo de Recoletos, which runs parallel to Serrano. When you reach Barbara de Braganza, turn left and walk up past the Plaza de las Salesas. A little way past the church on the right is Calle del Barquillo, an intriguing backstreet shopping area. Go all the way down until you come to the Calle de Alcalá. Turn right and, keeping to the right-hand pavement, walk along the Gran Vía as far as the metro station. Then turn left down Calle de Montera and you are back in Sol.

WEST FROM SOL

Start in the Puerta del Sol. Leave it at the western end and walk up Calle de Postas to Plaza Mayor. Cross the plaza and leave it at the diagonally opposite corner (El Arco de los Cuchilleros). At the bottom of the steps cross the street and go down Calle del Maestro de la Villa into the Plaza Conde de Barajas. Explore the streets in this area, and come up into the Plaza de la Villa.

Cross Calle Mayor and walk down as far as Calle San Nicolás. Go up it, past the church and into the Plaza Ramales. Continue down the side of the Plaza de Oriente to Calle Bailén, pausing for coffee at the Café del Oriente. Turn right and walk along the palace front. When you reach Calle San Quintin, there is a possible detour up to the Monasterio de la Encarnación.

With Plaza de Espana on your right, take the walkway under Calle Bailén, then walk up the steps to Templo de Debod, with its views of the Casa de Campo, the Royal Palace and the Almudena Cathedral. Descend the slope at the far end of Templo de Debod and cross the car park, from which a path goes down through the Parque del Oeste to the Rosaleda. When you get to Paseo del Rey, turn left and follow it as far as Cuesta de San Vicente. Go down to the Puerta de San Vicente and turn left into the Paseo de la Virgin del Puerto. On the left, about 150m down, you will find the entrance to the Campo del Moro, with the best views of the Royal Palace.

On exiting the park, continue along the Paseo de la Virgin del Puerto until you come to Calle Segovia, with the Segovia Bridge on the right. Follow Calle Segovia through the park until you come to the Arab Wall. Turn left off Calle Segovia up Costanilla de San Andrés, which will take you past the church and into Plaza de la Cebada, where there is a pleasant bar (El Viajero) at No. 11. Turn left and at Calle Toledo, turn left again. This leads back to Plaza Mayor and thence to Sol.

THE SIGHTS

- Puerta del Sol (➤ 35)
- Plaza Mayor (➤ 33)
- Plaza de la Villa (➤ 32)
- San Nicolás de los Servitas (➤ 55)
- Plaza de Oriente (➤ 30)
- Monasterio de la Encarnación (➤ 31)
- Templo de Debod (➤ 25)
- Parque del Oeste (➤ 25)
- Campo del Moro (➤ 29)
- Arab Wall (➤ 60)
- San Andrés (➤ 54)
- Plaza de la Cebada (➤ 52)

INFORMATION

Distance 8km
Time 4–5 hours
Start point Puerta del Sol
🚇 cll, D9
🚇 Sol (lines 1, 2, 3)
🚌 3, 5, 15, 20, 51, 52, 150
End point Puerta del Sol

EVENING STROLLS

MEDIEVAL MADRID

With its hilly, cobbled streets, medieval Madrid is best explored towards sundown. Starting in the Plaza de la Villa, walk southwards via Calle Puñorrostro into the Travesía del Conde. Looking south from here towards Calle Segovia, you will see the Plaza de la Cruz Verde, once used by the Inquisition for *autos de fe*. Crossing Calle Segovia, take the first small street to the right into the Plaza del Alamillo. You are now in the small area of atmospheric, winding streets known as the Morería, or Moorish quarter. From here, go to the Plaza de la Paja, and from there down the Costanilla de San Andrés to the Plaza de San Andrés. Walking up the Costanilla de San Pedro will bring you to the church of San Pedro el Viejo. Café del Nuncio, to the rear of San Pedro, is a lovely place for an early-evening *aperitivo*, particularly between April and October.

THE SALÓN DEL PRADO

Although many buildings in this area of Madrid can be visited during the day, many are also illuminated after sundown. Start in the Botanical Gardens, then walk up the centre of Paseo del Prado, past the Prado Museum as far as the Neptune Fountain in the Plaza Canovas del Castillo. Here turn right up the Calle de Felipe IV and turn right along the back of the Prado Museum to take in San Jerónimo el Real, hopefully illuminated. Continue up past Calle de Felipe IV and past the Cason del Buen Retiro on to Avenida de Alfonso XII. Opposite is the parterre entrance of the Retiro Park which is wonderful while there is still daylight, but should be avoided if there are no people around. Exit the park a little further north and go down Calle Antonio Maura to Plaza de la Lealtad. A little further on is the Neptune Fountain, from where you can either retrace your steps down the Paseo del Prado or cross it and walk up into the Santa Ana area for an evening drink.

The Gran Vía, meaning the 'Great Way', lit up

ORGANISED SIGHTSEEING

JULIA TOURS

Offers Artistic Madrid and Sightseeing Madrid Tours, and tours to the major sights in the surrounding area. The Scala Melía (➤82) has its own visit.

🚑 b1, D8 ✉ Gran Via 68 📞559 96 05 🕐 Mon–Sat 8–8; 8–noon 🚇 Santo Domingo

MADRID VISION & TRAPSATUR

Two companies operating from the same address. Madrid Vision runs five buses a day around all the major sights. Starting points include the Plaza de España (➤52), the Royal Palace (➤29), the Puerta del Sol (➤35) and the Calle Serrano (➤72). A ticket allowing you to get on and off as often as you wish in a day costs a little more than the ordinary tour price. Trapsatur offers half and full day tours. The 'Panorámica y Toros' takes in a bullfight during the bullfighting season. They also offer many excursions to locations such as Aranjuez and Chinchón (➤20), El Escorial (➤20), Segovia (➤21) and Toledo (➤21).

🚑 b1, D8 ✉ Calle San Bernardo 23 ☎ 541 6320/21 or 542 66 66 🚇 Santo Domingo

PATRONATO MUNICIPAL DE TURISMO

The Municipal Tourist Board provides Descubre Madrid (Discover Madrid) which offers all-year-round tours to many of the main sights, though few are in English.

🚑 b11, D9 ✉ Plaza Mayor 69 ☎ 588 29 00 🕐 Daily 8–3 🚇 Sol

PULLMANTOUR

Pullmantour offers an Artistic tour (Royal Palace (➤29), Calle Mayor (➤59), Puerta del Sol (➤35), Prado Museum (➤41)) and a Sightseeing Tour which visits the Parque del Oeste (➤25), Casa de Campo (➤57) and the Santiago Bernabeu football stadium amongst other sights. There are also excursions to Aranjuez and Chinchón (➤20), El Escorial (➤20), Segovia (➤21) and Toledo (➤21).

🚑 a111, C9 ✉ Plaza de Oriente 8 ☎ 541 1805/6/7 🚇 Opera

Made-to-measure sightseeing at low prices

For the more adventurous sightseer, armed with the appropriate map and guidebook, the Circular bus route (with its self-explanatory name) puts you within walking distance of many of Madrid's more important locations, and gives you a good idea of the different *barrios*, or areas, which make up the whole. Good pick-up points are in the Avenida Menéndez y Pelayo (near the Retiro Park), the Glorieta Emperador Carlos V (near the Prado Museum, the Reina Sofia and the Thyssen), and the Cuesta de San Vicente (near the Parque del Oeste). The round trip takes between 1 and 2 hours, depending on the traffic.

EXCURSIONS

ARANJUEZ & CHINCHÓN

Aranjuez was an attempt by the Spanish Bourbon monarchy to create a 'Spanish Versailles'. Inside the royal palace, particular highlights are the Porcelain Room, the Throne Room and the Smoking Room. The gardens were laid out in the 16th century and include a section called El Jardín de la Isla. A little further afield there is the immense Jardín del Príncipe (Prince's Garden), criss-crossed with tree-shaded walkways. At the far end stands the Casa del Labrador (Peasant's House) built for Charles IV. Nearby Chinchón has a 15th-century castle and a wonderful Plaza Mayor, lined with balconied houses. There is a Goya panel in the Assumption Church. Chinchón is the home of the anise liqueur named after it.

EL ESCORIAL

Philip II's vast architectural legacy built in the Doric style between 1563 and 1584. Measuring 205m from north to south and 160m from east to west, it contains 16 courtyards, 2,673 windows, 1,200 doors and 86 staircases; 900m of frescos line the walls. Its power is breathtaking, and the clear mountain air has kept its granite and blue slates looking extraordinarily new. Amongst its many highlights are the monastery, the library and the mausoleum, the resting place of most Spanish monarchs since Charles V. A little further north is the controversial Valle de los Caídos – General Franco's resting place and a monument to all those who died in the Civil War – which was built by Republican prisoners.

INFORMATION

Aranjuez and Chinchón
Distance 45km
Journey time 45 minutes
🕐 Mon–Fri 10–2, 3–5; Sat 10–2
🚌 ALSA from Estación Sur, Calle Canarias 17 (☎ 527 12 94)
🚆 Cercanías Line or the pleasant Tren de la Fresa (Strawberry Train ➤ 58)
💰 Expensive
ℹ️ Tourist Information Centre: Plaza San Antonio (☎ 891 04 27)

El Escorial
Distance 40km
Journey time 45 minutes
☎ 890 5903/4, 866 0238
🕐 Tue–Sun 10–6; Oct–Mar 10–5
🚌 Autocares Herranz, from outside Moncloa metro station. Buy your ticket here
🚆 Regular trains from Atocha
💰 Expensive
ℹ️ Last admission 1 hour before closing

Awe-inspiring El Escorial

SEGOVIA

Less touristy and more 'lived in' than Toledo, Segovia was founded during the Iberian period. It was taken in 80BC by the Romans and became the seat of a bishop under the Visigoths. Occupied by the Moors, it then reverted to the Christians in 1085, and a millennium later is a popular weekend haunt for *madrileños* who come in search of fresh air and a traditional suckling pig lunch. The first thing you see on entering the town is the Roman aqueduct (1st and 2nd centuries AD), with a total length of 813m, a maximum height of 128m and 165 arches. In the old town are the magnificent 16th-century cathedral, and the 14th-century Alcázar, or fortress, from the top of which there are lovely, airy views. A 15-minute walk takes you to a particularly tranquil spot from which to view the sunset and the Church of the True Cross.

Alcázar, the fortress at Segovia

TOLEDO

Toledo, one of the most beautiful and legendary cities in Spain, was the Spanish capital under the Visigoths (567–711), and from 1085 until 1561 when Philip II transferred the Spanish Court to Madrid. In other words, it has played a decisive role in Spanish history for far longer than Madrid itself. Between the 12th and 15th centuries Moors and Christians lived there side by side, and its rich combination of Christian, Moorish and Jewish legacies has led to the entire city being named a National Monument. It is a fascinating maze of winding streets and hidden patios, and its hilltop position affords wonderful views in every direction. Particular highlights are the magnificent 13th-century cathedral, the synagogue, the Casa de El Greco (the house of the Greek religious painter whose name is associated with the city) and the Alcázar, or fort, originally founded in 1085, which sits astride the town. To get the best out of Toledo, it is best to extend a visit over two days.

INFORMATION

Segovia

Distance 88km

Journey time 2 hours

 La Sepulveda bus line from Paseo de la Florida 11

From Chamartin station (very slow)

Candido, Plaza Azoguejo 5; Restaurante La Almuraza, Calle Marqués del Arco 3

Tourist Information Centre: Plaza Mayor 10 (☎ 921 460334). The office on Plaza Azoguejo offers information on the surrounding region

Toledo

Distance 50km

Journey time 1 hour

Galeano International from Estación Sur, Calle Canarias 17 (☎ 527 12 94)

From Atocha, several every hour

Tourist Information Centre: Puerta Bisagra ☎ 925 220843), on the north side of Toledo

WHAT'S ON

JANUARY	*Cabalgata de Reyes* (5 Jan): procession through streets to announce to Madrid's children the coming of the Three Wise Men
	San Antón (17 Jan): hundreds of people congregate in the San Antón Church, Calle Hortaleza 63, to have their pets blessed
FEBRUARY	*Carnival week* before Lent, with processions and parties. Ends on Ash Wednesday with the ritual known as the Burial of the Sardine by the River Manzanares
	ARCO (dates variable): international contemporary arts festival
APRIL	*Semana Santa* (Holy Week): processions of hooded, shoeless, chain-dragging *penitentes*, who bear images of Christ and the Virgin on their shoulders. On Holy Thursday during the procession around La Latina, the entire *barrio* takes to the streets
	International Theatre festival
MAY	1–2 May are public holidays. There is a concert in the Plaza 2 de Mayo
	San Isidro (15 May): the week leading up to the saint's day of Madrid's patron, San Isidro, is centred around the Plaza Mayor, with nightly performances. On the Sunday before the 15th, a huge *cocido* (Madrid's traditional dish) is served, with everyone wearing traditional dress. This is the most important part of Madrid's bullfighting year
AUGUST	*Verbenas*: (open-air saint's day celebrations) in the area around La Latina and Lavapiés, in which the *barrio popular* takes to the streets until the small hours
SEPTEMBER–NOVEMBER	*Festival de Otoño* (Autumn Festival): an international performing arts festival which takes place at several different venues
SEPTEMBER–OCTOBER	*Música en las Ventas*: national and foreign contemporary musical acts in the bullring
DECEMBER	Annual *Feria de Artesanía* (crafts fair) in the Paseo de Recoletos
	In the weeks leading up to Christmas, the Plaza Mayor hosts its Christmas fair.
	New Year's Eve: thousands of *madrileños* gather in the Puerta del Sol to see the fireworks and eat one grape for each of the clock's 12 chimes

MADRID's
top 25 sights

The sights are shown on the maps on the inside front cover and inside back cover, numbered **1–25** *from west to east across the city*

1

ERMITA DE SAN ANTONIO

"Goya is the painter whom most madrileños would wish to claim as their own. The San Antonio Hermitage is the finest monument which the city could have raised to his memory."

History Though a little off the beaten track, the two churches are well worth a visit, both for their small-scale intimacy and for Goya's frescos, restored in 1990. The original hermitage was begun in 1792 by Charles IV's Italian architect, Francisco Fontana, on the site of a previous hermitage. Goya's remains were buried here in 1919, unfortunately without his head: rumour has it that it was stolen by scientists who wished to study it. A National Monument.

The frescos The frescos were painted using a technique which was revolutionary at the time and it is the richness of their colours which most attracts the attention. They tell the life of Saint Anthony, representing the saint raising a murdered man from the dead to enable him to name his murderer and thus save the innocent accused. The models for the frescos were members of the Spanish Court, but include other, less reputable figures – which has been seen as indicating Goya's contempt for the Court of the time.

Girlfriends and boyfriends The San Antonio Hermitage is considered by *madrileños* to be particularly *castizo* (of the people), and there attaches to it a peculiar ritual which is still carried out today. Saint Anthony is the patron saint of boyfriends; every 13 June, girls go to the Hermitage to pray that they will find a boyfriend. Thirteen pins are placed inside the font; when the girls put their hands into the font, the number of pins which stick to their hands indicates the number of boyfriends they will have that year.

HIGHLIGHTS

- Cupola
- Balustrade
- Marble and stucco font (1798)
- Lápida de Goya
- Mirrors under the cupola
- High altar
- Lamp under the cupola (18th century)
- *Inmaculada* by Jacinto Gómez Pastor
- *San Luis and San Isidro*, Jacinto Gómez Pastor

INFORMATION

- B8
- Glorieta de San Antonio de la Florida 5
- 542 07 22
- Tue–Fri 10–2, 4–8. Sat and Sun 10–2. Closed Mon and public hols
- Norte
- 41, 46, 75
- Norte Station
- None
- Cheap. Free Wed and Sun
- Parque del Oeste (➤ 25)
- Guide book sold at entrance

PARQUE DEL OESTE

❝Less frequented and more informal than the Retiro, the Parque del Oeste is the best place in the city for a peaceful, twilight summer stroll, particularly at its quieter northern end.❞

History Originally designed in the first years of this century by landscape gardener Cecilio Rodríguez on what had previously been an immense rubbish dump, the Parque del Oeste was practically destroyed during the Civil War as it was a front against the Nationalist troops invading Madrid. In its rebuilt form it is still, despite the best efforts of litter louts and graffiti artists, one of the city's most appealing and romantic open spaces. The park contains birch, fir, atlas cedar and cypress trees amongst others, as well as a 17,000sq m rose garden, La Rosaleda, which is host to a rose festival each May, and several statues including, in the Paseo de Camoens, the 1952 Juan Villanueva fountain. There is a *teleférico* (cable car) in the park which runs out to the Casa de Campo, affording bird's-eye views over the west of Madrid. During the summer, elegant, noisy terrace bars are set up along the Paseo de Pintor Rosales, which was Ernest Hemingway's favourite street.

Templo de Debod It is somehow typical of Madrid that one of its oddest and most interesting attractions should not be Spanish at all; the Debod Temple is at the southern corner, near Plaza de España, in a little park of its own on the site of a former military barracks. It is a 4th-century Egyptian temple honouring the god Amon. It was installed in 1970 as a gift from the Egyptian government to Spanish engineers and archaeologists who had saved many valuable artistic treasures before large areas of land were flooded by the construction of the Aswan dam.

HIGHLIGHTS

- Templo de Debod
- *Teleférico*
- La Rosaleda
- Fuente
- Statue of Juan de Villanueva
- Statue of Sor Juana Inés de la Cruz
- Statue of Simón Bolívar
- View over Casa de Campo
- Trees, including atlas cedar, cypress and magnolia

INFORMATION

- B7
- Jardines del Paseo del Pintor Rosales
- 908 614 53/ 409 61 65
- (Templo de Debod): Tue–Fri 10–2, 6–8;. Sat and Sun 10–2. Closed Mon and public hols
- Plaza de España, Ventura Rodríguez, Moncloa
- 74, 84, 93
- Templo de Debod: Cheap. Free Wed and Sun
- Ermita de San Antonio (► 24)

Top: the Debod Temple

MUSEO DE AMÉRICA

INFORMATION

- ✚ C6
- ✉ Avenida Reyes Católicos 6
- ☎ 543 94 37
- 🕐 Tue–Sat 10–3; Sun and public hols 10–2.30. Closed Mon
- Ⓜ Moncloa
- 🚌 Circular, 82, 83, 84.
- 💰 Cheap. Free Sun
- ♿ Excellent

Vessel from Peru

"An attractively set-out museum and the best place in Spain in which to obtain a flavour of the culture of a different continent."

History Situated on the edge of Madrid's sprawling University City area, the America Museum is devoted to the presentation and explication of Pre-Columbian and Hispanic artefacts from Latin America. As such it makes a unique contribution to Spanish cultural life; depending on your point of view, it can be seen either as an attempt to promote international understanding or as propaganda for the Spanish Conquest. The collection was housed in part of the Archaeological Museum until 1993, when it took its present form. Tragically, much of the material brought back between Columbus's first voyage and the mid-17th century was destroyed in successive palace fires, and more of the exhibits were brought back to Spain by scientists, or given as donations, than by the *conquistadores*.

Layout The only information in English is a small pamphlet available at the entrance. The collection is spread over two floors and it is advisable to follow the suggested route. It contains five areas with different themes: Area 1 is called 'The Tools of Understanding'; Area 2 'The Reality of America'; Area 3 'Society'; Area 4 'Religion'; and Area 5 'Communication'. Audio-visual aids are available for those who speak Spanish. Two particular highlights are the Treasure of the Quimbayas, with skull-cap helmets, drinking flasks, trumpets etc from Columbia, and the Trocortesiano Maya codex which records the arrival of the Spaniards in the New World in minute, intricate runes.

MUSEO CERRALBO

❝*Idiosyncratic and intermittently splendid, the Cerralbo is a lesson in how the nobility of Madrid in general lived one hundred years ago, and of the extravagant personality of the Marquis de Cerralbo in particular. A real curiosity.***❞**

History Seen from outside, the two-storey, late 19th-century home of the 17th Marquis of Cerralbo – politician, man of letters and collector – looks rather unpromising. It is the only house-museum in Madrid in which the rooms themselves, ranging from the magnificent to the frankly shabby, steal the show from the fascinating clutter of artefacts on display. The Marquis donated the house and its contents to the state in 1922, stipulating in his will that his collection should be displayed exactly as he had left it. Unless you collide with a school group, there are not likely to be many people. You are given an explanatory pamphlet at the entrance, and guides indicate the best route to follow.

The collection After entering, there is a magnificent grand staircase by Soriano Fort to the right. On the first floor the most notable exhibit is El Greco's striking *Ecstasy of St Francis* (1600–5), which hangs in the chapel. In the gallery surrounding the patio there are works by Ribera, Alonso Cano and some haunting Magnasco landscapes. On the second floor there are collections of Western and oriental weaponry, a dining-room containing a remarkable Snyders painting, and an appealingly cosy library, but pride of place is given to the sumptuous, mirrored ballroom. The Marquis also had a taste for Saxon porcelain and intricately engineered clocks: the enormous mystery clock in the ballroom is a fascinating artistic paradox.

HIGHLIGHTS

- Grand staircase
- *Ecstasy of St Francis*, El Greco
- *Jacob with his Flock*, Ribera
- *Devotion*, Alonso Cano
- *Immaculate Conception*, Zurbarán
- *Porcupines and Snakes*, Snyders
- Sword collection from the courts of Louis XV and XVI
- Porcelain Room
- Ballroom
- Monumental mystery clock in ballroom

INFORMATION

- ✚ C8
- ✉ Calle Ventura Rodríguez 17
- ☎ 547 36 46
- 🕐 Tue–Sat 9:30–4:30; Sun 10–2. Closed Aug and public holidays
- Ⓜ Ventura Rodríguez, Plaza de España.
- 🚌 1, 46, 74, 75
- 💲 Cheap. Free Sun and Wed
- ↔ Parque del Oeste (▶25)
- ♿ Few

Top: the Salón de Baile

5

CATEDRAL LA ALMUDENA

INFORMATION

"Though not the world's prettiest cathedral, it symbolises the laid-back attitude of the madrileños to what should have been one of their highest priorities. I find its mixture of styles an intriguing record of years of architectural thought."

A long delay Incredible though it may seem, until 1993 Madrid lacked a cathedral, the San Isidro Church laying unofficial claim to the title. The story of the Almudena is one of procrastination: the crypt alone took 30 years to complete. Constructed on what was formerly the site of Muslim Madrid's principal mosque, the first plans for the Almudena were drawn up in 1879 under Alfonso XII by the architect Sacchetti. Redesigned in 1883, it is based on the pattern of a 13th-century cathedral, with a chancel similar to the one at Rheims. A neo-classical style was introduced into the design in 1944 by Sidro and Chueca, but financial problems delayed completion of the cloister until 1955, with the façade following five years later. The final touches were not added until 1993, when the cathedral was finally consecrated by the Pope. The main entrance is opposite the Royal Palace, while the crypt is along La Cuesta de la Vega.

The story of the Almudena Virgin According to legend, the image of the Virgin over the entrance had been hidden by Mozarabs (Jews and Christians living under Moorish rule). When El Cid reconquered Madrid, he ordered that the image be found, but without success. When Alfonso VI arrived in Madrid, he instructed his troops and the people of Madrid to dismantle the city walls to find the image. When they reached the grain deposits, they heard a noise from the turrets above, which then collapsed, revealing an image of the Virgin and Child.

6

PALACIO REAL (ROYAL PALACE)

"I find the sheer pomp a little overwhelming. The story that sentries guarding the rear of the building used to freeze to death in the icy wind adds to the sense of chilliness it inspires. However, the scale is undeniably awesome."

History The Royal Palace (also known as the Palacio de Oriente or the Palacio Nacional) was begun under Philip V in 1737 after the old Muslim fortress had been destroyed by fire in 1734. The original design by Juvara was for façades measuring 476m each, or three times longer than the palace as it is now, but there was neither the space nor the money for it. It was not completed until 1764, with the new, reduced design being completed by Sacchetti. From the street side, it is a normal palatial building of the period, with Doric pilasters framing the *piano nobile* windows. The royal family does not actually live here: it is used occasionally for state visits, during which dinner is served in the Gala dining-room. The entrance is to the south side of the building, across the Plaza de la Armería, which is flanked by the Royal Armoury housing El Cid's sword and suits of armour.

Interior and gardens Inside the Palace, there are more than 3,000 rooms, most of which are never used. The only way to see the palace is by a guided tour of the most impressive rooms, reached by a grand staircase with a ceiling by Conrado Giaquinto. The Sala de Gasperini has a remarkable stucco ceiling, while the Sala de Porcelana, built for Charles III, has a fine display of white, gold and green porcelain plaques. To the north of the palace are the elegant Sabatini Gardens, which offer the best view of the palace, while to the rear is the Campo del Moro (Moor's Field) where there is a splendid Carriage Museum.

HIGHLIGHTS

- Grand staircase
- Sala de Porcelana
- Salón de Alabarderos, with tapestries from 1760
- Salón de Columnas
- Saleta de Gasparini
- Salón de Carlos III
- Clock collection
- Chapel by Sacchetti and Ventura Rodríguez
- Music Museum
- Sabatini Gardens

INFORMATION

- ✚ all, C9
- ✉ Calle Bailén
- ☎ 542 00 59
- 🕐 Mon–Sat 9:30–5;. Sun and public hols 9–2
- Ⓜ Opera
- 🚌 3, 25, 33, 148
- 💰 Moderate. Free Wed
- ↔ Catedral la Almudena (► 28)
- ♿ Very good

Philip II, by the Royal Palace

MADRID
A
FELIPE II

7

PLAZA DE ORIENTE

DID YOU KNOW?

- General Franco held mass rallies here
- Tunnels beneath the square date back to Moorish times
- Earliest royal with statue: King Ataulfo (AD 415)
- Statue of Philip IV is at the geometrical centre of square
- Previous location of Philip IV was Buen Retiro Palace
- Statues brought to square in 1841
- First performance in Royal Theatre was Donizetti's *The Favourite*
- Equestrian statue weighs 7,500kg

INFORMATION

- all, C9
- Plaza de Oriente
- Café de Oriente
- Opera
- 3, 25, 33
- Palacio Real (➤ 29), Monasterio de la Encarnación (➤ 31)

❝An aperitivo *on the terrace of the Café de Oriente, with the harmonious gardens stretching away in front of you to the Royal Palace, is undoubtedly the best place to reflect on the might of the monarchy at the height of its powers.*❞

Ambitious emperor Currently under restoration, the elegant Plaza de Oriente was planned in 1811 under Joseph Bonaparte. To build it, he had to destroy the monuments and churches which then surrounded the Royal Palace. His aim was to build a kind of Champs Elysées, running from the Plaza to the Cibeles Fountain. Fortunately, perhaps, the project was abandoned; had it not been, Madrid would have lost, amongst many other treasures, the Convent of the Royal Shoeless Nuns. The existing square dates from the reign of Isabel II. The gardens contain statues of the kings and queens of Spain, which were originally intended for the top of the Royal Palace facing on to the plaza, but they were too heavy. Queen Isabel II apparently had a dream in which an earthquake caused them to topple over on to her.

Royal Theatre At the eastern end of the square stands the Royal Theatre, built between 1818 and 1850. It was closed in 1987, but may reopen shortly. The site had previously been occupied by an open-air theatre, but in 1737 it was extended for a visit by Farinelli, the legendary *castrato*, of whom Philip V was particularly fond. It opened that year on the Saint's Day of Isabel II, its founder.

The horse In the centre of the square there is an equestrian statue. It is of Philip IV by Montañés, taken from a portrait by Velázquez and cast in Florence by Pietro Tacca.

MONASTERIO DE LA ENCARNACIÓN

"Located away from the traffic of Calle Bailén, the Monastery of the Incarnation could be called the monumental equivalent of a tranquilliser. The atmosphere of religious calm brings peace to the soul."

History Designed by Juan Gómez de Mora in 1611 under instructions from Queen Margarita, wife of Philip III, the church in the Royal Monastery – still used by nuns of the Augustine order – is the lesser-known of Madrid's two monastery museums (the other being the Descalzas Reales). It is a typical example of Habsburg Spanish religious architecture. At the time it was connected to the Arab fortress (where the Royal Palace now stands) by a secret passage. Damaged by fire in 1734, and reconstructed by Ventura Rodríguez in a classical-baroque style in the 1760s, the granite façade is all that remains of the original. A 45-minute guided tour leads you through the intricacies of the monastery, going via the Royal Room (with fairly uninspired portraits of the Spanish royal family), by way of one of Madrid's most beautiful churches, and ending at the Reliquary.

The Reliquary At the centre stands an altar and altar-piece with a panel depicting the Holy Family by Bernadino Luini, a pupil of Leonardo da Vinci. On the altar there is a beautifully ornate tabernacle in bronze and rock crystal. Inside is a crucifix of Christ with a crown of thorns, oddly charred: convent tradition holds that this is what remains of a crucifix which was defiled and burnt by heretics. Amongst the 1,500 relics on display, which include a good many bone fragments, the most noteworthy is to the right of the door as you enter: in a small glass globe is the dried blood of St Pantaleón which mysteriously liquefies from midnight every 27 July, St Pantaleón's Day.

HIGHLIGHTS

- *John the Baptist,* Jusepe Ribera
- *Handing over of the Princesses,* anonymous painting in lobby
- *Recumbent Christ,* Perronius
- Royal Room
- Altar-piece
- Cupola, with frescos by González Velázquez
- Frescos: Francisco Bayeu
- Charred crucifix
- Blood of St Pantaleón

INFORMATION

- al, C8
- Plaza de la Encarnación 1
- 542 00 59
- Wed and Sat 10:30–2.30, 4–5:30. Sun 11–1:30
- Opera
- 3, 148
- Cheap. Free Wed
- Catedral la Almudena, Palacio Real (▶28, 29)
- None

9

PLAZA DE LA VILLA

HIGHLIGHTS

- Statue of Admiral Alvaro de Bazán
- Staircase of Honour (Casa del Ayuntamiento)
- Statue of Goya (Casa del Ayuntamiento)
- Visiting Room, with engraving of oldest map of Madrid (1622) (Casa del Ayuntamiento)
- Glass patio (Casa del Ayuntamiento)
- Tapestry Room, with 15th-century pieces (Casa de Cisneros)
- Commissions Gallery

INFORMATION

- ✚ all, D9
- ✉ Plaza de la Villa
- ☎ 588 29 06/08
- ◷ Buildings open Mon 5–6
- Ⓜ Sol, Opera
- 🚌 3
- 💲 Free
- ↔ Plaza Mayor, Puerta del Sol (► 33, 35)
- ❓ Spanish guide only for buildings. With advance phone call, guided tours in French and English can be arranged for groups
- ♿ None

❝*Its small scale, with its three architectural styles huddled together in harmonious co-existence, makes a pleasant change from some of the more imposing buildings in Madrid. If you come upon it accidentally at night, as I did, the memory will linger.***❞**

Casa del Ayuntamiento This typically Castilian and perfectly rectangular square, dramatically floodlit at night, is home to three separate buildings in different styles. Originally the site of an Arab street market, it was the venue for Madrid Town Council meetings from 1405, a function it continues to serve to this day. The Casa del Ayuntamiento (sometimes referred to as la Casa de la Villa) is Castilian-baroque and was designed in 1640 by Juan Gómez de Mora (who brought rectangular forms to the Madrid landscape), with two doors, one for the Council and one for the prison, for which purpose the building also served. The existing doors are baroque modifications, dating from 1670. The building's façade was later altered by Juan de Villanueva in 1787, and a balcony leading on to the Plaza Mayor was added. Inside, there is a grand staircase and a room containing a painting by Goya.

Two more buildings The Casa de Cisneros, on the south side of the square, is one of Madrid's finest examples of the Plateresque style that was prevalent in the 16th century, although it has been much restored. It dates back to 1537. The Torre de los Lujanes is one of the few monuments in Madrid surviving from the 15th century; it is a fine example of late Gothic civic architecture. It is said that King Francis I of France was held prisoner here for a while in 1525 by Hernando of Alarcón, who was the owner of the house at the time .

PLAZA MAYOR

❝The Plaza Mayor strikes a chord with everyone entering it for the first time: it's now that you fully realise that you are in the capital of Spain. Surely it is only in Madrid that the recent frescos on the Casa Panadería could have survived.**❞**

History Built in the 15th century as a market square, and later renamed the Plaza del Arrabal (Square outside the Walls), the Plaza Mayor came into its own when Philip II, after making Madrid the capital of Spain, ordered it to be rebuilt as the administrative centre of the Court. The only part to be completed at the time was the Panadería, or the bakery (the frescos are the work of the last ten years), while the rest of it was completed in 1619 by architect Juan Gómez de la Mora under Philip III, whose bronze equestrian statue (by Juan de Bolonia and Pietro Tacca) stands at the centre. It was reconstructed after the Civil War by Juan Cristóbal. A fire in 1790 meant that much of the square had to be rebuilt. The buildings between the towers on either side of the square are Town Hall offices; the rest are highly desirable private residences.

A gathering place During the 17th century, the Plaza Mayor was where the more important members of the Court lived. At the end of the 17th century, the square became the site for bullfights, carnivals and the terrible *autos de fe* of the Spanish Inquisition, which were attended by thousands on 30 June 1680, when 118 of the offenders were executed in a single day. Hangings were carried out here until the end of the 18th century. To this day the cobbled expanse of the Plaza is the scene for many public gatherings.

DID YOU KNOW?

- Number of arches: 114
- Number of balconies: 377
- Square measures 120 x 90m
- Shop at No. 4 opened in 1790
- Seven 'Juans' have played a part in the square's history
- Three destructive fires, in 1631, 1672 and 1790
- Philip II statue was gift from Duke of Florence
- Official name of square is Plaza de la Constitución

INFORMATION

- ✚ bII, D9
- ✉ Plaza Mayor
- 🍴 *Terraza* bars around square
- Ⓜ Sol
- 🚌 3, 5, 150
- ↔ Plaza de la Villa (➤ 32)
- ❓ Tourist Office in square

Where better to watch the world go by

11

CONVENTO DE LAS DESCALZAS REALES

HIGHLIGHTS

- *Recumbent Christ*, Gaspar Becerra
- *Neapolitan Nativity* (Chapel of St Michael)
- *Virgin of the Forsaken*, Tomás Yepes
- *St Ursula and the Eleven Thousand Virgins*, Giulio Lucini
- Bust of the *Mater Dolorosa*, José Risueño
- *Cardinal Infante Don Fernando of Austria*, Rubens
- *The Ship of the Church*, 16th-century painting
- *Adoration of the Magi*, Brueghel
- *The Empress Maria*, Goya
- Church

INFORMATION

- bl/II, D9
- Plaza de las Descalzas Reales 3
- 542 00 59
- Tue, Wed, Thur, Sat 10:30–12:45, 4–5:45; Fri 10:30–12:45; Sun and public hols 11–1:45
- Sol, Callao
- 3, 5, 150
- None
- Moderate. Free Wed
- Puerta del Sol, Real Academia de Bellas Artes de San Fernando (➤ 35, 36)

Top: Recumbent Christ, *by Becerra*

❝*Though the tour of the Royal Shoeless Nuns' Convent is conducted at a frenetic pace, the building contains an unusually high proportion of unmissable treasures and is worth more than one return trip.*❞

'A vile stink' Of Madrid's two monastery museums, the Descalzas Reales – oddly located in the centre of commercial Madrid – is the richest. It is a small miracle that it has managed to remain intact; most of its rooms are small museums in themselves. Founded on the site of the palace in which Juana of Austria – the younger daughter of Charles V, and its foundress – was born, it was built in Madrid brick, between 1559 and 1564 by Antonio Silla and Juan Bautista of Toledo, with the church being completed in 1570 by Diego de Villanueva. The whole place breathes an air of mid-17th-century religious mysticism, though the 'vile stink' of which traveller William Beckford complained when attending Mass here in the late 18th century has thankfully now departed. The original sisters were all of noble or aristocratic blood, and each founded a chapel on reception into the order: there are 33 of them, and to this day the convent is home to 33 Franciscan nuns, each of whom is responsible for maintaining one of the chapels.

The art collection The tour of the convent takes in a quarter of the rooms. Given in Spanish only, it lasts around 45 minutes and is conducted at such a frenzied pace that it is worth buying a guide book at the entrance. The church can only be visited during Mass, at 8AM or 7PM. The Grand Staircase, with its *trompe l'oeil* portrait of Philip IV and his family standing on the balcony, is covered with frescos by the artist Claudio Coello.

PUERTA DEL SOL

"Sol is the city's barometer: some twenty minutes spent wandering around here with your eyes and ears open might not give you a very good sense of the city, but an excellent one of the people who live in it."

Heart of Madrid Puerta means 'gateway', but the gateway was demolished in 1570 when the square was widened to receive Anne of Austria, Philip II's fourth wife. Almost inevitably during a stay in Madrid you will cross the square several times. For many *madrileños*, it is the true heart of the city. The design of the present square dates back to 1861, but the building on the south side, the Casa de Correos, is from 1768. Originally the Post Office, it is now the headquarters of the Madrid regional government. Spain's Kilometre Zero can be found on the pavement in front of it. The clock and tower were built in 1867, and each year thousands of *madrileños* gather beneath it to see in the New Year.

A troubled history It was in Sol that the Esquilache mutiny of 1766 began, sparked off by Charles III's uncharacteristically tyrannical insistence that the population should wear short capes and three-cornered hats. The most notable moment in its history was on 2 and 3 May 1808, when the *madrileños* took up arms against the invading French troops, a heroic but doomed attempt in which more than 2,000 died. Both days are immortalised in Goya's two magnificent anti-war paintings in the Prado. Various 20th-century uprisings took place in Sol: in 1912 politician José Canalejas was assassinated, and the Second Republic was proclaimed here in 1931.

HIGHLIGHTS

- Mariblanca statue
- Bear and *madroño* (strawberry tree) statue
- Statue of Charles III
- La Mallorquina pastry shop
- Newspaper stands: a major part of Madrid street-life
- Tío Pepe sign ('Andalusian Sunshine in a Bottle')
- Kilometre Zero
- Doña Manolita's lottery ticket stalls

INFORMATION

- cll, D9
- Puerta del Sol
- Sol
- 3, 5, 15, 20, 51, 52, 150
- Plaza Mayor, Convento de las Descalzas Reales, Real Academia de Bellas Artes (▶ 33, 34, 36)

Statue of the bear with a strawberry tree

35

13

REAL ACADEMIA DE BELLAS ARTES

HIGHLIGHTS

- Goya self-portraits (Room 2)
- *The Burial of the Sardine,* Goya (Room 2)
- *Alonso Rodriguez,* Zurbarán (Room 3)
- *Christ Crucified,* Alonso Cano (Room 3)
- *Head of John the Baptist,* Ribera (Room 4)
- *Felipe IV,* Velázquez (Room 4)
- *Susana and the Elders,* Rubens (Room 8)
- *Spring,* Arcimboldo (Room 8)
- *Martyrdom of S Bartolome,* Ribera (Room 23)
- Goya etchings (Calcografia Nacional)

INFORMATION

- ✚ cll, D9
- ✉ Calle Alcalá 13
- ☎ 522 14 91
- 🕐 Tue–Fri 9–7; Sat Sun Mon and public hols 9–2:30
- Ⓜ Sol, Sevilla
- 🚌 3, 5, 15, 20, 51, 52, 150
- 💰 Cheap. Free Sat and Sun
- 🔁 Convento de las Descalzas Reales, Puerta del Sol (► 34, 35)
- ♿ None

❝ *Though often passed over in favour of the big three – the Prado, the Thyssen and the Reina Sofia – the stately and graceful Royal Academy of Fine Arts is well worth a visit. Rarely overcrowded, it is small enough to be visited comfortably in a couple of hours.* **❞**

History 'Following those in Rome, Paris and Florence and other great cities', as the painter Francisco Meléndez expressed it when he suggested the idea, the Royal Academy originated with Philip V in 1744, and was seen through to its conclusion by Fernando VI in 1752. The Academy was originally housed in the Casa de la Panadería, in the Plaza Mayor, but Charles III transferred it to its present site in 1773. In 1972 the building was closed for general reorganisation, and reopened in 1986. The original building was baroque, but shortly after it opened, Academy members with conservative tastes insisted that it be toned down and given the neo-classical façade we see today.

Layout The museum has three floors and its layout is not consistent with chronology. The best-known exhibits are on the first floor, with Room 2 (Goya), Rooms 3 and 4 (Spanish 17th century), Room 8 (Flemish and Italian masters) and Room 9 (Renaissance works) particularly worth lingering over, while Room 12 contains work painted by artists seeking to enter the Academy. It is worth paying particular attention to Arcimboldo's *Spring* in Room 8, as this is the only Arcimboldo in Spain and one of only a handful in the world. Half-way up the stairs to the entrance (and easily missed) is another museum, La Calcografía Nacional, or Engraving Plates Museum. At the back of this is the Gabinete Goya, a hidden treasure which contains a beautifully displayed series of the original plates used by the artist for his etchings.

COLECCIÓN THYSSEN-BORNEMISZA

❝*This is one of the best things that has happened to Madrid since the end of the Civil War, as well as being one of the few internationally renowned art museums in which* **everything** *is worth seeing.***❞**

A new museum The Thyssen, housing what may be the world's finest private art collection, first opened its doors to the public in October 1992. The collection was technically on loan to Spain, but in the face of stiff competition from the likes of Prince Charles and the Getty Foundation, a final agreement to purchase it was reached in June 1993, with the Spanish state paying out $350 million. The collection was begun by Baron Thyssen's father; after his death in 1947 the paintings were dispersed among his heirs, but his son bought them back. Continuing to collect himself, and also wishing to keep the collection together, he and his wife 'Tita' Cervera (a former Miss Spain), chose the Palacio de Villahermosa.

The collection The sheer variety of the 775 works on display has caused some to call the Thyssen over-eclectic; others reply that its very quirkiness is part of its charm. Each room specialises in a different period, with the top floor devoted to medieval to 17th-century art, the first floor to rococo and neo-classicism through to fauvism and expressionism, while the ground level features surrealism, pop art and the avant-garde – so it is best to start from the top and work your way down. A free guide book is provided.

King Henry VIII *by Holbein* (1497–1543)

HIGHLIGHTS

- *Portrait of Giovanna Tornabuoni*, Ghirlandaio
- *Portrait of Henry VIII*, Holbein
- *St Catherine of Alexandria*, Caravaggio
- *Annunciation Diptych*, Van Eyck
- *St Jerome in the Wilderness*, Titian
- *The Lock*, Constable
- *Easter Morning*, Caspar David Friedrich
- *Les Vessenots*, Van Gogh
- *Houses on the River*, Egon Schiele
- *Man with a Clarinet*, Picasso

INFORMATION

- ✚ dll, E9
- ✉ Paseo del Prado 8
- ☎ 420 39 44
  Information 369 01 51
- 🕐 Tue–Sun 10–7
- 🍴 Café, restaurant ££
- Ⓢ Banco de España
- 🚌 1, 2, 5, 9, 10, 14, 15, 20, 27, 34, 37, 45, 51, 52, 53, 74, 146, 150
- Ⓔ Atocha, Recoletos
- 🔲 Moderate
- ↔ Museo del Prado (▶41)
- ❓ Bookshop on ground floor
- ♿ Excellent

15

CENTRO NACIONAL DE ARTE REINA SOFÍA

HIGHLIGHTS

- View from exterior lifts
- Enclosed patio
- *Guernica*, Picasso
- Juan Gris Room
- Picasso Room
- Miró Room
- Dalí Room
- Surrealism Room
- Luis Buñuel Room
- Spanish 20th-Century Art Room

INFORMATION

- ✚ dIV, E10
- ✉ Calle Santa Isabel 52
- ☎ 467 50 62/468 30 02
- ◷ Daily 10–9; Sun 10–2:30. Closed Tue
- 🍴 Bar, restaurant (££)
- Ⓜ Atocha
- 🚌 6, 10, 14, 24, 26, 27, 32, 34, 36, 37, 41, 45, 47, 54, 56, 57, 85, 86
- 🚉 Atocha
- 💲 Cheap. Free Sat afternoon and Sun morning
- ↔ Estación Atocha
- ❓ Excellent shop on ground floor
- ♿ Very good

Top: Picasso's Guernica
Above: external lifts on the Reina Sofía

❝You might not like all the works on display, but even on its busiest days the Reina Sofía Museum, with its light, space and air, offers you somewhere to be alone for contemplation.❞

A triumph of planning Inspired by the Pompidou Centre in Paris, this is Madrid's finest contemporary art centre. The museum became a permanent exhibition space in 1990. Indeed, within Europe only the Pompidou surpasses its 12,505sq m of exhibition space. Transparent lifts on the exterior of the building whisk you up glass tubes to a thrilling view over the rooftops of Madrid. The

museum houses a permanent collection on the second floor, which is devoted to 20th-century Spanish art, with all its 'isms' – Cubism, Surrealism, Realism, Informalism. Most of the other space is devoted to a (sometimes radically avant-garde) programme of temporary exhibitions.

Guernica Picasso's masterpiece dominates the Reina Sofía. When it was originally commissioned by the Republican Government for display at the 1937 Paris Exhibition, their only instruction to Picasso was to paint something big: it measures 3.5 by 7m. Taking his inspiration from the Nationalist bombing of the Basque town of Guernica in 1937, this huge painting has become the great anti-war symbol of 20th-century art. The decision in 1995 to remove the bullet-proof screen was seen by many as a symbolic gesture, showing that democracy in Spain had finally taken root.

MUSEO SOROLLA

"*A beautifully serene spot, which communicates the successful effort of one artistic soul to create for himself an oasis of peace in a busy city.***"**

Entrance and gardens Built in 1910–11 by Enrique María de Repollés, the Sorolla Museum is the best of Madrid's house museums, and one of the few places in the city to give us a sense of the shape of an artist's life and work. It was the Madrid home of Spain's finest impressionist painter, Valencian Joaquín Sorolla (1863–1923). It was converted into a museum after Sorolla's wife Clotilde donated it to the state, and it was first opened to the public in 1932. The two small gardens, designed by Sorolla himself as a setting for his collection of fountains and fonts, are a little bit of Andalucía in Madrid: the first is an imitation of a part of the Seville *alcázar*, while the second is modelled on the Generalife Gardens in Granada's Alhambra. Near the entrance is a replica of a white marble bust of Sorolla by Mariano Benlliure, and to the left, opposite the entrance, there is an Andalucian patio area.

The house Lovingly preserved, the house is divided over two floors into seven rooms, a salon area and a dining-room, with each room given over to a different aspect of Sorolla's work. This has divided critics, some of whom see his art as having a fairy-tale, picture-postcard quality, but there is no denying the brilliance of Sorolla's use of light, and his eloquent reflection of a leisurely, idyllic world before World War I, in which everyone wears white, the sea continually sparkles in the sunlight, young women lie decorously on the grass reading books, and there is no need to be unduly passionate about anything at all.

HIGHLIGHTS

- *La Bata Rosa* (Room II)
- *Self Portrait* (Room III)
- *Clotilde en traje de noche* (Room III)
- *Clotilde en traje gris* (Room III)
- Turkish bed, used by Sorolla for siestas (Room III)
- *La Siesta* (Room IV)
- *Las Velas* (Room IV)
- *Nadadores* (Room V)
- *Madre* (Room VI)
- New York gouaches (Drawings Room)

INFORMATION

- ✚ E7
- ✉ Paseo del General Martínez Campos
- ☎ 310 15 84
- ◷ Tue–Sat 10–3; Sun and public hols 10–2
- ◉ Iglesia, Rubén Darío
- ◻ 5, 7, 16, 40, 61, 147
- ◔ Cheap. Free Sun
- ♿ Few

17

PLAZA DE LA CIBELES

❝ *Madrid's most overwhelming plaza, though the sheer mass of fashioned stone might be a little hard to stomach. Sadly, the constant traffic means it cannot be enjoyed as it deserves.* **❞**

History The statue of La Cibeles, the fertility goddess, is Madrid's equivalent of the Eiffel Tower. Seated imperiously at one of Madrid's busiest intersections, the sea goddess and her marble fountain were erected according to instructions from Charles III by Francisco Gutiérrez (responsible for the main statue) and Robert Michel (the lions, whose names are Hipponomes and Atlanta). It was completed in 1792 and originally stood at a corner of the square. The cherubim were added in 1895.

Around the Plaza The enormous wedding-cake look-alike on the south-eastern side of the square is one of Madrid's most imposing buildings. Visitors are sometimes disappointed to discover that it is only the Central Post Office – often referred to by local wits as 'Our Lady of Communications'. It was designed by Antonio Palacios in 1904, with a painstakingly worked façade reminiscent of the Viennese style.

The Palacio de Linares The real treasure of the Plaza de la Cibeles is the Palacio (which is said to be haunted). It was designed in 1872 by architect Carlos Collubi, though it was restored and opened again in 1992 as the Casa de América. The well-lit interior is now a showcase for the visual arts of Latin America. The Palacio was opened as a gesture of goodwill on the 500th anniversary of Columbus's discovery of America; regular temporary exibitions are held there. The garden is elegantly laid out, and during the summer there is a snack bar.

Top: Central Post Office
Above: La Cibeles statue

MUSEO DEL PRADO

❝ *The city's pride in the Prado Museum is justified. Magnificent, frustrating, and magnificently frustrating, it is one of the world's great museums, its dazzling reputation manifested by a certain haughty indifference to visitors.* **❞**

Brief history There are people who still believe that Madrid is a 'one-sight city', and that that sight is the Prado's art collection. The neo-classical building, completed by Juan de Villanueva in 1785, was originally conceived by Charles III as a centre for the study of natural sciences. After being damaged by Napoleon's troops during the Spanish Wars of Succession, it was restored by Fernando VII as a home for the royal collection of paintings and sculptures. It was opened as a museum in November 1819 and is a National Monument. The collection it houses – 7,000 pictures, of which around 1,500 are on display – is unequalled in the world. This number includes 115 Goyas, 83 Rubens, 50 Velázquez, 40 Brueghels, 36 Titians, 32 El Grecos and 20 Zurbaráns. Like all great museums, the Prado is best appreciated by making more than one visit. The main entrance is the Puerta de Goya, at the northern end.

***Las Meninas, Las Majas* and the 'dark paintings'** Do not leave the Prado without making sure you have seen Velázquez's masterpiece, *Las Meninas*, which is considered by many to be quite simply the best painting in the world. Goya's *Majas* – two paintings of (perhaps) the Duchess of Alba, one clothed, one naked – are Madrid's own 'Mona Lisas'. His *pinturas negras* were painted near the end of his life, and are obviously the work of a man whose sanity is in decline. Grotesque, disturbing and breathtaking, they are unique.

HIGHLIGHTS

- *Las Meninas*, Velázquez
- Goya's 'dark paintings'
- *The 2nd of May, The 3rd of May, Las Majas*, Goya
- *The Holy Family*, Raphael
- *The Bacchanal, Emperor Charles V in Mühlberg*, Titian
- *The Garden of Delights*, Bosch
- *The Triumph of Death*, Brueghel
- *Self Portrait*, Dürer
- *David and Goliath*, Caravaggio
- *The Three Graces*, Rubens

INFORMATION

- dll/lll, E9
- Paseo del Prado
- 420 36 62/420 37 68
- Tue–Sat 9–7; Sun 9–2
- Banco de España
- 1, 2, 5, 9, 10, 14, 15, 20, 27, 34, 37, 45, 51, 52, 53, 74, 146, 150
- Atocha, Recoletos
- Cheap. Free Sat after 2:30 and free Sun
- Plaza de Cibeles, Archaeological Museum (▶ 40, 43)

Top: Goya's La Maja Desnuda

41

19

SAN JERÓNIMO EL REAL

HIGHLIGHTS

- Chapels
- 19th-century altar-piece by José Méndez
- 19th-century wooden pulpit
- Organ in choir, gift from Queen Maria Cristina
- Stained-glass windows
- Bronze hanging lamps

INFORMATION

- ✚ E9
- ✉ Calle Moreto 4
- ☎ 420 30 78
- ◷ Daily 8–1:30, 5–8:30
- Ⓠ Banco de España, Retiro
- ▣ 10, 14, 19, 27, 34, 37, 45
- ▤ Atocha
- ▦ Free
- ↔ Museo del Prado (▶41)
- ❓ Information telephone to right of entrance
- ♿ None

"_This rather odd-looking hybrid has a certain solid power, and is a breathtaking sight if happened upon during a night-time stroll._**"**

A royal church Also called 'Los Jerónimos', this Gothic church, with its single nave and chapels between the buttresses, has long been favoured by the Spanish monarchy as both the location for official ceremonies and for spiritual retreat. Founded on the banks of the River Manzanares in 1464 by Henry IV as the San Jerónimo el Real Convent, it was moved to its present site and rebuilt in 1503 for Ferdinand and Isabel, the Catholic monarchs. It was here that every prince of Asturias, from Philip II in 1528 to Isabella II in 1833, was sworn in. Los Jerónimos was the site of the marriage between Alfonso XIII to Victoria of Battenberg in 1906, and the present king, Juan Carlos I, was crowned here in 1975. During the reign of Philip IV it was connected to the Casón del Buen Retiro by underground passages. The building was badly damaged during the Napoleonic Wars in 1808, but restoration carried out between 1848 and 1883, during which towers and pinnacles were added, has done much to preserve the flavour of the original.

The Salón del Prado The monastery grounds once encompassed a part of Madrid which occupied the area set back from the Paseo del Prado between the Carrera de San Jerónimo and the Calle de Alcalá. San Jerónimo was the centre-piece of the part of the Salón known as the Huerta de los Jerónimos, or the Jerónimos Orchard. Together with the Prado of Atocha, it made up an area called the Salón del Prado, designed by Hermosilla under instructions from Charles III after 1767, and was in the shape of a race-track, with the two parallel avenues ending in a semicircle.

Top: detail from stained glass window

PALACIO DE BIBLIOTECAS Y MUSEOS

"A spacious and well-lit treasure trove, the National Library and Museum takes us to the heart of why Spain is what it is today."

The building The huge Palacio de Bibliotecas y Museos, with its impressive neo-classical façade and eight-columned portico, was completed in 1892 to commemorate the 400th anniversary of the discovery of America, and is home to the National Archaeological Museum and the Spanish National Library (founded by Philip III).

Archaeological Museum The entrance is at the rear of the building on Calle Serrano. Under the garden, there is a peculiar reproduction of one of the oldest cave paintings in Europe, the depiction of a herd of bison, found at Altamira. The museum is a beautifully laid-out collection which is as valuable artistically as it is archaeologically, taking us through from prehistory up to (oddly for an archaeological museum) the 19th century. It is large enough for visitors to be able to avoid the school parties. Its chief attractions are the Iberian Dama de Elche and the Visigothic votive Guarrazar Crowns.

Library The library houses 3 million volumes, to which 120,000 are added every year. On the approach to the building there are statues of Alfonso X the Wise, Cervantes and other well-known historical and literary figures. Though none of the books are on display, the library does contain a 22,000-strong collection of the texts which have shaped Spanish literary history, including a 14th-century manuscript of El Cid. Temporary exhibitions are also held here.

Top: the Archaeological Museum
Right: the library

HIGHLIGHTS

- Amenemhat sarcophagus (Room 13)
- Dama de Ibiza (Room 19)
- Dama de Elche (Room 20)
- Sculpture of Livia (Room 21)
- Sundial (Room 23)
- The Guarrazar Crowns (Room 29)
- Alaferia Arches (Room 30)

INFORMATION

- ⊞ E8
- ✉ Serrano 13
- ☎ 577 79 12
- ⏰ Tue–Sat 9:30–8:30; Sun and public hols 9:30–2:30
- Ⓜ Serrano, Colón
- 🚌 5, 14, 21, 27, 37, 45, 53
- Recoletos
- Cheap. Free Sat afternoon and Sun
- Jardines del Descubrimiento (►44)
- ♿ None

21

JARDINES DEL DESCUBRIMIENTO

HIGHLIGHTS

- Statue of Christopher Columbus
- Tableaux set in base of statue
- Water curtain
- Inscriptions on statues
- Skateboarders
- City Cultural Centre
- Map on wall of Cultural Centre
- Botero statues

INFORMATION

- E8
- Plaza de Colón
- Cafeteria Restaurante del Centro Cultural
- Colón
- 1, 5, 9, 14, 19, 21, 27, 37, 45, 51, 53, 74, 89
- Recoletos
- Archaeological Museum (➤ 43)

"Though not perhaps particularly beautiful, the Discovery Gardens are certainly impressive, and I include them as an example of more recent architectural developments in Madrid."

1970s Madrid Typical of Madrid town-planning concepts of the 1970s, these 52,000sq m gardens, which are located in the Plaza de Colón, were built to celebrate Spain's role in the discovery of the New World. The gardens are dominated by an indifferent statue of Christopher Columbus by Jerónimo Suñol, which faces west towards the Americas. This was a wedding gift from the Spanish nobility to Alfonso XII. Underneath the gardens is the Centro Cultural de la Villa de Madrid, protected from the chaos of the outside world by a deafening curtain of water. When working, the fountain in the centre of the Plaza de Colón is the most beautiful in Madrid, but it has been under repair for four years.

The statues The Columbus statue is 17m high, on a base with four tableaux representing scenes from Columbus's life (Queen Isabella offering him jewels, Columbus narrating the story of his grand project). But it is the wonderful macrosculptures from 1977, the work of Joaquín Vaquero Turcios, which hold the eye. The decision to locate them in such close proximity to the more classically oriented statues further along Paseo de la Castellana

Detail (top) on the Columbus statue (above)

caused controversy at the time. The three statues represent Columbus's three ships – the *Pinta*, the *Niña* and the *Santa María* – as they sail across the Atlantic in 1492 towards the fourth statue, which represents the New World. The effect is best appreciated from the end of Lake Serrano.

PUERTA DE ALCALÁ

"*If you are brought to the centre of Madrid from the airport by taxi, this is one of the first things you will see. Though Madrid is not generally thought of as a city of great monuments, the Puerta de Alcalá gives the lie.***"**

History Listed as a National Monument, recently restored to its former glory and located in the Plaza de la Independencia, the Puerta de Alcalá, together with Cibeles, is one of the great symbols of Madrid. Situated along the line of the old city walls, it is perhaps the city's finest example of the neo-classical architecture which came as a reaction to previous baroque excesses. It was designed by Francisco Sabatini in 1778 as the main entrance to the Court and was commissioned by Charles III, who was to be responsible for so much of the city's architectural transformation. Five previous designs had been rejected. The bullet-marks from the 1921 assassination attempt on Eduardo Dato, the President of Madrid's Council of Ministers, can still be seen on the north side of the statue. Best appreciated when floodlit at night, the Puerta de Alcalá unfortunately stands at the centre of an immense traffic junction.

Design Made up of five arches of granite and stone, the statue's ten columns – facing east, and crowned with Ionic capitals – are similar to those by Michelangelo for the Capitol in Rome. There are three central archways, with two smaller ones at the sides. The lion heads in the centre of the three higher arches are the work of Robert Michel, and the cherubim, the trophies and the coat of arms which surmount the statue are by Francisco Gutiérrez. Several years ago the idea came to an enlightened member of the Madrid Town Council to paint parts of the *puerta* white. Luckily, the idea was rejected.

DID YOU KNOW?

- A bullring stood near the site until 1873
- The Puerta is 22m high (not including shield)
- Middle arches are 10m high
- Subject of a pop song by Ana Belén

INFORMATION

- E8
- Plaza de la Independencia
- Retiro
- 9, 19, 15, 20, 28, 51, 52, 74
- Recoletos
- Plaza de la Cibeles (➤ 40)

PARQUE DEL RETIRO

HIGHLIGHTS

- Palacio de Cristál
- Artichoke Fountain in the Rose Garden
- Cecilia Rodriguez Gardens
- Velázquez Palace
- Statue of Alfonso XII
- Lake
- *Fallen Angel* statue
- 400-year-old cypress tree near Philip IV entrance
- Philip IV parterre
- Observatory (1790)

INFORMATION

- E/F9, 10
- Calle Alcalá, Alfonso XII, Avenida de Menedez Pelayo, Paseo de la Reina Cristina.
- *Terrazas*
- Retiro, Atocha, Ibiza
- 2, 14, 19, 20, 26, 28, 68, 69
- Atocha
- Colección Thyssen-Bornemisza, Museo del Prado, Puerta de Alcalá (▶ 37, 41, 45)

"Small enough to feel at home in, and large enough to get pleasantly lost in, the Retiro Park is sure to remain in the memory, particularly if seen in the late spring or early autumn when its colours are at their most vivid."

History The best time to visit the Retiro is on a sunny Sunday afternoon, when the city is drawn to it as if by instinct. Originally thickly wooded, and once a hunting ground for Philip II, this 1.2sq km space in the heart of the city was the brainchild of the Duke of Olivares, who designed it in the 1630s for Philip IV as part of the Buen Retiro Palace – a complex of royal buildings and immense formal gardens, which was later to be the inspiration for Louis XIV at Versailles, and which was used until the time of Carlos III. Retiro means 'retreat'. Most of the palace was destroyed during the Napoleonic Wars.

A walk in the park Enter from opposite the Casón del Buen Retiro on Calle Alfonso XII. Walk through the parterre gardens and up the steps along a broad, tree-shaded avenue until you come to the lake; if you want to take a boat out, then head round the lake towards the left. Opposite you is a statue of Alfonso XII, a popular spot for baking in the sun. Otherwise, turn right and follow the lake round; just beyond where the water ends, turn left and you will come to the Palacio de Cristál (Glass Palace), the Retiro's loveliest building, constructed of iron and glass. Continuing in a straight line will bring you to La Rosaleda or Rose Garden. From here, a left turn will take you to the statue of the Fallen Angel (the Devil), or a right turn to the Cecilia Rodríguez Gardens. A left turn at the end of the gardens will bring you to the Velázquez Palace, which regularly hosts art exhibitions.

24

MUSEO LÁZARO GALDIANO

"A memorable experience: there cannot be many museums like this, still unfamiliar to many madrileños. *A wonderful oddity, tiresome and stimulating by turns, but every time I go I discover a new favourite."*

A born art collector An obsessive, seemingly unfocused collector of art, who died in 1948 at the age of 80, Galdiano was born into the nobility in Navarre. He married Paola Florido, an Argentinian who shared his affinity for art, and together they devoted their lives to travelling round the world in search of artistic treasures which they would snap up on no better advice than their own taste. An essentially private man, Galdiano never revealed how much he paid for any of the masterpieces. On his death, he donated his collection to the state and, despite its unevenness, it surely comprises one of the world's greatest private collections. It includes work by Bosch, Murillo, Rembrandt, Zurbarán, El Greco, Velázquez, Ribera, Turner and Goya, as well as exquisite gold and silverwork, Russian enamelwork, pieces of jewellery, fans, rock crystal and weaponry.

Pleasure and pain A good example of the kind of mansions the late 18th-century *madrileño* aristocracy built along the Paseo de la Castellana, the museum opened its doors to the public in 1951. A visit to this three-storey, 30-room museum, the neo-classical Parque Florido Palace, can demand patience. The paintings have been left hanging in the often individualistic order on which Galdiano insisted; many of them are unnumbered; the only guide available is in Spanish and 300 pages long; there is nowhere to sit and the lift rarely works. None of this stops it from being easily the finest of Madrid's smaller art galleries.

HIGHLIGHTS

- *The Virgin of Charity,* Caravaggio (Room 11)
- *Landscape,* Gainsborough (Room 12)
- *Saint John in Patmos,* Bosch (Room 20)
- *Portrait of Saskia van Uylendorch,* Rembrandt (Room 21)
- *Luis de Góngora,* Velázquez (Room 23)
- *The Adoration of the Magi,* El Greco (Room 23)

INFORMATION

- F6
- Serrano 122
- 561 60 84
- Tue–Sun 10–2. Closed Aug
- República Argentina/ Nuñez de Balboa
- 12, 16, 19, 51, 89
- Cheap
- None

Top: The Adoration of the Magi *by El Greco*

Below: the Parque Florido Palace

25

Plaza de Toros (Bullring)

"Whatever your feelings about this particular aspect of Spanish culture – is it art or bloodsport? – you cannot help but be impressed by the scale of the Plaza. It is obviously best appreciated during the spectacle of a bullfight."

History and architecture Officially opened in 1934, this is perhaps the world's most important bullring, the place in which a bullfighter must triumph if he is to achieve international recognition in the bullfighting world. It is also Madrid's finest example of neo-Mudéjar, an architectural style which resurfaced during the 19th century in imitation of the Mudéjar architecture of the 13th and 14th centuries, and is defined by an interesting use of brickwork and bright, inlaid ceramic tiling. In the square in front of the bullring there is an over-the-top statue in memory of bullfighter José Cubero, inscribed with the deathless words 'a bullfighter died, and an angel was born'.

Museo Taurino Half an hour spent in the rather stuffy Museo Taurino (it is located next to the stables), which was renovated recently, is sufficient to give you a basic idea of some of the famous names of bullfighting, if not of the complex art of bullfighting itself. Massive heads of legendary bulls and portraits of great bullfighters line the walls, and there are several dramatic portrayals of bull-runs, particularly the one by Mariano Benlliure. The highlights are the 'suits of lights', including one belonging to Juanita Cruz, an early 20th-century woman bullfighter who was never allowed to fight on Spanish soil, and that of Manolete, perhaps the greatest of them all, which he was wearing on his death in 1947.

Bull fight poster

MADRID's *best*

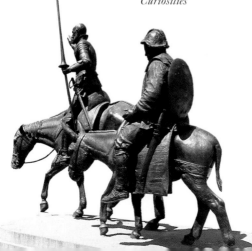

MUSEUMS & GALLERIES

Some tips

Museo in Spanish is not the same as 'museum' in English, but means both 'museum' and 'non-commercial art gallery' – hence the 'Museo del Prado'. Madrid is particularly well served with *museos*, several of which are unknown to the locals. These are divided into the state and the privately run, with the privately run generally having better facilities and staff attention – although at present very few of them have facilities for non-Spanish speakers.

ANTHROPOLOGICAL MUSEUM
Also called the Ethnological Museum, this four-storey building was Spain's first museum of its kind. Although it cannot claim to be comprehensive, it contains some fascinating material, exhibited in galleries devoted to different geographical areas. Of special interest are the skeleton of a 2.28m man from Badajoz, the Zairean masks, and the shrunken heads from the Amazon. There is also a rather elegant Inuit anorak made from seal intestines.

➕ E10 ⊠ Calle Alfonso XII 68 ☎ 539 59 95 ◷ Tue–Sat 10–7:30; Sun, public hols 10–2. Closed Mon 🚇 Atocha, Atocha RENFE 🚌 10, 14, 27, 34, 37, 45 💷 Cheap ♿ None

CASÓN DEL BUEN RETIRO
Originally the ballroom of the Buen Retiro Royal Palace, this building was destroyed by Napoleonic troops but then rebuilt by Charles III, who instructed Luca Giordano to decorate the vault with frescos. Today it is an annexe to the Prado containing the 19th-century Spanish art collection. A Prado entrance ticket is valid here.

➕ E9 ⊠ Calle Alfonso XII 68 ☎ 420 26 28/420 06 70 ◷ Tue–Sat 9–7; Sun 9–2 🍴 Yes 🚇 Retiro G19 💷 Cheap; free on Sat and Sun afternoon ♿ Very Good

Fresco in the Casón del Buen Retiro

JUAN MARCH FOUNDATION
One of Europe's most important private art foundations, and home to around 30 major exhibitions a year which are often amongst the most interesting to be found in Madrid; these have included exhibitions of Picasso, Kandinsky and Matisse. The permanent collection is largely made up of contemporary Spanish art.

➕ F7 ⊠ Calle Castelló 77 / Calle Padilla 36 ☎ 435 42 40 ◷ Mon–Sat 10–2, 5:30–9; Sun and public hols 10–2. Closed Aug and between exhibitions 🚇 Nuñez de Balboa 🚌 29, 52 💷 Free ♿ Very good

MUSEO DE LA CIUDAD (MUSEUM OF THE CITY)

Opened in 1992, this spacious four-storey museum is a hi-tech equivalent of the Museo Municipal, and at every step there is the odd sense of seeing Madrid repeating itself in miniature. The museum explains in almost numbing detail the workings of Madrid's transport, telephone and water systems, but it also has some attractive scale models and lots of interactive displays.

F6 Calle Príncipe de Vergara 140 588 65 77 Tue–Fri 10–2, 4–6; Sat–Sun 10–2 Cruz del Rayo 29, 52 Free Guided tours can be arranged in advance Excellent

MUNICIPAL MUSEUM

Built between 1721 and 1729 on the site of an old hospice, the Municipal Museum traces the history of Madrid through archaeological discoveries, paintings and maps, with some lovely landscape paintings showing an older, greener, city. It contains works by Bayeu, Carducho and Goya – a dramatic allegory of Madrid amongst others – as well as a striking model of the city constructed in 1830. The fine baroque doorway is by Pedro Ribera, the outstanding architect of Madrid's Golden Age.

d8 Calle Fuencarral 78 588 86 72 Tue–Fri 9:30–8; Sat–Sun 10–2. Closed Mon and public hols Tribunal 149 Cheap; free on Wed and Sun None

NATURAL SCIENCE MUSEUM

Built in 1881, this is one of Madrid's first buildings to use glass and metal on a grand scale. In the modern section – on the left as you face it – there is a circular room displaying hunting trophies and stuffed animals which are not for the faint-hearted, and a variety of audio-visuals. In the older section there is the museum's prize piece, *Megatherium americanum*, brought back from Argentina in 1788, and the first extinct animal ever to be scientifically classified. Particularly odd is the astronaut hanging next to the monkeys.

E6 José Gutiérrez Abascal 2 411 13 28 Tue–Fri 10–6; Sat 10–8; Sun and public hols 10–2 Nuevos Ministerios 14, 27, 40, 147, 150 Cheap Few; steps up to entrance

ROMANTIC MUSEUM

This monument to faded romantic glory, in urgent need of restoration, is inside a typical mid-18th-century *madrileño* building which was the home of the traveller and painter, the Marquis of Véga-Inclán. Though the contents here might be too sentimental for some tastes, there are many items of interest, particularly Alenza's miniature *Satires of Romantic Suicide*, Goya's *Saint Gregory the Great* and a collection of Isabelline and Imperial furniture.

E8 Calle San Mateo 13 448 10 45 Tue–Sat 9–3; Sun and public hols 10–2. Closed Aug Tribunal 21, 37 Cheap; free on Sunday Very good

Closures

It is unlikely that all the sections of all the museums in Madrid have ever been open simultaneously. Redecoration and renovation are necessary evils, and can cause frustration, especially since any enquiry as to when they will reopen is likely to be met by a shrug of the shoulders. Many of the museums are closed on Mondays.

Outside the Casón del Buen Retiro

PLAZAS

Places of celebration

The plaza, or square (whether round or oblong) is central to a Spaniard's conception of his environment. The plazas have always been focal points where the community gathers, particularly to celebrate; they still have that function today. It is worth checking at metro stations for advertisements for any event due to take place in a plaza. Even if you might not understand what is going on, there is sure to be a good atmosphere.

PLAZA DE CASCORRO

In the heart of the *barrio popular* of old Madrid, this plaza is at the top end of the fabled Rastro street market. *Rastro* means 'trace', thus the area is named after the traces of blood left by animals on their way to the slaughterhouse which once stood near by. It is a perfect place to experience the hustle and bustle of the Old Quarter on a late Sunday morning. On the right stands Los Caracoles, a long-standing seafood bar which is typical of the area. Just down Calle Ribera de Curtidores, there is a statue of local hero Eloy Gonzalo, while at the top of Calle Embajadores there is an immense mural depicting the Rastro as it was one hundred years ago.

➕ bIII, D9 ✉ Plaza de Cascorro 🚇 La Latina, Tirso de Molina 🚌 17, 23, 35

PLAZA DE LA CEBADA

One of the more authentic squares, it retains its name even though it no longer looks like a square. The Cebada market (opened 1875) was Madrid's first example of iron architecture; before the market, bullfights were held here. At the beginning of the 19th century, it was the scene of public executions.

➕ bIII, D9 ✉ Plaza de Cascorro 🚇 La Latina, Tirso de Molina 🚌 17, 23, 35

PLAZA DE LAS CORTES

This is the home of the Congreso de los Diputados, or parliament buildings. The entrance is guarded by two bronze lions (popularly known as Daoíz and Velarde after the heroic captains of the Napoleonic invasion), whilst the cannons were brought back from the African War in 1860. An attempted military *coup* took place inside the building in 1981, and was recorded on video for posterity. There are weekly guided tours of the interior.

➕ dIII, E9 ✉ Plaza de las Cortes 🚇 Sevilla 🚌 5, 150, N5, N6

PLAZA DE ESPAÑA

This grandiose, slightly daunting square has a statue of Cervantes at its western end, overlooking a rather lovable 1815 statue of his two legendary creations, Don Quixote and Sancho

Crowds gather in the city's plazas as religious processions pass by

Panza. The Edificio España, with its neo-baroque doorway, was Madrid's first true skyscraper, while the functional Torre Madrid, which is 137m high, was Europe's tallest building at the time of its construction in 1957, and a symbol of post-Civil War economic recovery.

🟦 C8 ✉ Plaza de España Ⓜ Plaza de España 🚌 68, 69, 74, 133

PLAZA DE LA LEALTAD
A stone's throw from the Prado, and dominated by the Ritz Hotel, this elegant, semicircular plaza also contains an obelisk to the memory of those who died at the hands of Napoleonic troops on 3 May 1808. Their ashes are kept in an urn at the base of the monument. The Madrid Stock Exchange was built here in 1884, to a neo-classical design which neatly echoes that of the Prado.

🟦 dII, E9 ✉ Plaza de la Lealtad Ⓜ Banco de España 🚌 10, 14, 27, 34, 37, 45

PLAZA DOS DE MAYO
This is the heart of the historic *barrio* of Malasaña, which today is best known for its slightly run-down, disreputable atmosphere, though it is being renovated. Manuela Malasaña and her daughter became heroes during the invasion of Napoleonic troops on 2 May 1808. In the square there is a statue of the two captains who participated in the battle, Daoiz and Velarde.

🟦 D8 ✉ Plaza 2 de Mayo Ⓜ Bilbao 🚌 21, 147

The statue of Cervantes in the Plaza de España

PLAZA DE LA PAJA
During the period of Muslim rule, this pleasant little square was the site of the most important *zoco*, or street market; during the Middle Ages it housed desirable aristocratic residences. Of the many palaces which were located here, the most notable is at No 14, the Lasso de Castilla Palace, which was the preferred residence of the Catholic kings when they stayed in Madrid. It is now extremely unpalatial in appearance.

🟦 aIII, C9 ✉ Plaza de la Paja Ⓜ La Latina 🚌 3, 31, 148

PLAZA DE SANTA ANA
Once occupied by the Santa Ana monastery, the plaza today is surrounded by bars and is a perfect place in summer for watching the world go by. There is a statue of playwright Calderón de la Barca in the centre, and at the eastern end stands the Teatro Español, built in 1849 after the original building, an open-air theatre, was gutted by fire.

🟦 cII, D9 ✉ Plaza de Santa Ana Ⓜ Sol, Sevilla 🚌 5, 150

Executions in the Plaza de la Cebada
Public executions took place in Madrid until the early years of this century. The instrument of death was the *garrote vil*, a particularly nasty metal instrument which was screwed around the neck and tightened until the neck broke. Most famous among the many criminals executed in the Plaza de la Cebada was Luis Candelas, the popular bandit, in 1837.

53

CHURCHES

The bell of San Pedro el Viejo

'St Peter's the Elder' is so called to distinguish it from another St Peter's of more recent construction. According to legend, the bell on arrival was so large that it could not be taken up to the bell-tower, and was left leaning against the walls overnight. The following morning it had mysteriously raised itself into the tower. The miracle led to the belief that the bell had magical powers, such as the ability to ward off thunderstorms. The bell was removed in 1565.

Tip: it is generally best not to visit churches during Mass, other than for religious purposes.

CONVENTO DE SAN ANTÓN

Designed by Pedro Ribera and built by Juan de Villanueva, this example of baroque architecture houses a magnificent art collection, of which the highlights are Goya's *The Last Communion of Saint José de Calasanz*, painted between 1775 and 1780, and Ventura Rodríguez's *Dolphins* statue.

✚ E8 ✉ Hortaleza 63 ☎ 521 74 73 🚇 Tribunal, Chueca

SAN ANDRÉS

The undoubted highlight of this National Monument is the Capilla del Obispo (Bishop's Chapel) which was built between 1520 and 1530 and reflects the transition between Madrid's Gothic and Renaissance periods. The nave and apse have Gothic vaulted ceilings, while the decorative aspects are Renaissance. There is a particularly fine wooden altar-piece carved by Francisco Giralta, while the paintings above it are by Villoldo el Mozo. The dome over the sanctuary of the San Andrés Chapel dates from the end of the 15th century.

✚ alII, CD9 ✉ Plaza de San Andrés 1 ☎ 365 48 71 🚇 Mon–Sat 8–12:30; do not visit during Mass. Closed Sun and public hols 🚇 La Latina, Tirso de Molina 🚌 3, 148 ♿ None

SAN FRANCISCO EL GRANDE

Built between 1761 and 1784, with a neo-classical façade by Francisco Sabatini and an immense, overwhelming 33m dome by Miguel Fernández. The monastery here was used as a military barracks from 1835, after which it was lavishly redecorated. The interior contains much work by Spanish masters, including an early Goya, *The Sermon of San Bernadino de Siena* – in the first chapel on the left. There is also a museum.

✚ alII, C9 ✉ Plaza de San Francisco ☎ 365 38 00 🚇 Tue–Sat 11–1, 4–6:30. Closed Sun and Mon 🚇 La Latina, Tirso de Molina 🚌 3, 7, 60, 148 ♿ None

Santa Bárbara, in Calle Bárbara de Braganza

SAN ISIDRO

San Isidro is the patron saint of Madrid, and between 1885 and 1993 – until the completion

of the Almudena – this immense baroque church was Madrid's unofficial cathedral. Built in 1620 by Pedro Sánchez for the Jesuits, the church was commandeered by Charles III after he expelled them. San Isidro's remains, which had until then been in San Andrés, were brought here.

The basilica of San Francisco el Grande

✚ blII, D9 ✉ Calle Toledo 37–39 ☎ 369 20 37 🚇 La Latina 🚌 17, 23, 35 ♿ None

SAN NICOLÁS DE LOS SERVITAS

Madrid's oldest church. Though much restored after the Civil War, San Nicolás's tower is one of the very few echoes in the city of Arabic Madrid. Designated as a National Monument, it is probably the minaret of a mosque which was later consecrated as a church. Its 12th-century tower is Mudéjar (built by Moslems under Christian rule), while the central apse is Gothic. Juan de Herrera, employed by Philip II as the architect of El Escorial, was buried in the crypt in 1597.

✚ all, C9 ✉ Plaza de San Nicolás 6 ☎ 559 40 64 🕐 Mon 9–1.30. Do not visit during Mass. Not always open; advance phone call advisable 🚇 Opera, Sol ♿ None

SAN PEDRO EL VIEJO

Noteworthy principally for its 14th-century Mudéjar tower and the legends surrounding it, San Pedro stands on the site of an old mosque. In the doorway are the only coats of arms extant from the period preceding the Catholic monarchs. Part of the interior is from the 15th century, while the rest is largely of 18th-century construction.

✚ a/blII, D9 ✉ Calle Nuncio 14 ☎ 365 12 84 🕐 8–12:30. Do not visit during Mass 🚇 La Latina, Tirso de Molina ♿ None

SANTA BÁRBARA (LAS SALESAS REALES)

Probably the grandest, if not the most attractive, of Madrid's churches, Las Salesas, was built by order of Bárbara de Braganza, the wife of Fernando VI. It has an elaborate façade built between 1750 and 1758 by Carlier and Moradillo, and contains Sabatini's tomb of Fernando VI (1713–59). It is currently the home of the Palacio de Justicia, or Supreme Court.

✚ E8 ✉ Calle Bárbara de Braganza 3 🚇 Alonso Martinez, Colón

MONUMENTS & STATUES

Madrid's gateways

The *puertas*, or gateways of Madrid are one of its distinguishing features. Each of them was built to mark the end of one of the highroads into the city. The Puerto de Toledo, the gateway to the city from the royal road from Andalucia, was completed in 1827 having been begun by Joseph Bonaparte in 1813. It was to be the last of Madrid's gateways. They are at their best when illuminated at night.

Botero's Hand in the Castellana

56

See Top 25 Sights for
JARDINES DEL DESCUBRIMIENTO (➤44)
PUERTA DE ALCALÁ (➤45)

BOTERO STATUES
In 1994, a section of Castellana was devoted to an exhibition by Fernando Botero. When the exhibition ended, *madrileños* were asked which of the sculptures they would like to keep. They chose a *Hand* in the middle of Castellana; the *Reclining Woman* in Calle Génova; and *Man on a Mule* in the Plaza de Colón.
➕ E8/E6 ✉ Colón. Plaza de San Juan de la Cruz 🚇 Colón. Nuevos Ministerios 🚌 7, 14, 27, 40, 147, 150

FALLEN ANGEL (RETIRO PARK)
The 'fallen angel', of course, is Lucifer: *madrileños* will tell you that this is the world's only statue in his honour. It is by Ricardo Bellver and dates from 1881.
➕ F9 ✉ Retiro. Glorieta del Angel Caido 🚇 Atocha 🚌 19, 20

FUENTE DE LOS DELFINOS
Housed in the San Antón convent on Calle Hortaleza, the *Dolphins* statue is the work of Ventura Rodríguez.
➕ E8 ✉ Calle Hortaleza 63 ☎ 521 74 73 🚇 Tribunal, Chueca 🚌 3, 7 ♿ None

FUENTE DE LA FAMA
The Ribera Gardens, to the rear of the Municipal Museum, have been turned into a children's playground, but the fountain by Pedro Ribera remains a delight.
➕ D8 ✉ Jardines del Arquitecto Ribera, Calle Barceló 🚇 Tribunal 🚌 21, 37, 40, 48

FUENTE DE NEPTUNO
In the Plaza de Cánovas de Castillo, the Neptune fountain by Ventura Rodríguez shows the King of the Sea riding a carriage in the shape of a shell, pulled by two horses.
➕ dII, E9 ✉ Plaza de Cánovas del Castillo 🚇 Banco de España 🚌 10, 14, 27, 34, 37, 45

MUSEO DEL ARTE CONTEMPORÁNEO AL AIRE LIBRE
Connecting the Calles Juan Bravo and Eduardo Dato is a walkway over the Paseo de la Castellana. Underneath is an open-air sculpture display with work by many of Spain's best-known contemporary artists.
➕ EF7 ✉ Paseo de la Castellana 🚇 Rubén Darío 🚌 5, 14, 27, 37, 45

PARKS & GREEN SPACES

See Top 25 Sights for
PARQUE DEL OESTE (►25)
PARQUE DEL RETIRO (►46)

BOTANICAL GARDENS

These gardens are the result of expeditions overseas, dating back to the 18th century, which went in search of interesting species. The plants and trees are carefully classified and laid out along geometrical walkways. The gardens are a haven of peace, best visited in spring or autumn.

➕ E9 ✉ Plaza de Murillo 2 🚇 Atocha 🚌 10, 14, 27, 34, 37, 45

CASA DE CAMPO

If you include the 1,723-hectare Casa de Campo in your calculations, then Madrid becomes the greenest city in Europe; it is possible to walk for a couple of hours without being interrupted. The park contains sports facilities and a large recreational lake, the Leisure Park and the *teleférico* (cable car) which runs up to the Parque del Oeste.

➕ B8/9 ✉ Calle Marqués de Monistrol, Avenida de Portugal 🚇 Lago, Batán 🚌 41, 33, 39, 65, 75, 84

FUENTE DEL BERRO

This intricate little 17th-century landscape garden, just south of the bullring and, unfortunately, too near the M30 motorway, is something of a well-kept secret. The attractive Berro fountain is like a little piece of jungle in Madrid. There is plenty of shade in summer and several eye-catching statues.

➕ H8 ✉ Alcalde Sainz de Baranda 🚇 O'Donnell 🚌 15

LOS CAPRICHOS DE ALAMEDA DE OSUNA

This is the closest Madrid comes to a formal English garden. Though a fair distance from the centre, it is a pleasant place for a Sunday stroll.

✉ Avenida de la Alameda de Osuna 🚇 Canillejas

JARDINES DE LAS VISTILLAS

The best place in Madrid from which to watch the sunset, with wonderful views over the Casa de Campo towards the Guadarrama mountains. From late spring to autumn, Las Vistillas is a lively place to go in the evening to enjoy a drink.

➕ C9 ✉ Travesía Vistillas 🚇 Opera. La Latina 🚌 3, 148

A green city

Technically, Madrid is Europe's greenest capital city, but this is mainly because of the vast 1,723-hectare Casa de Campo, 'the lungs of Madrid', which stretches away to the north-west. At night many of the parks attract drug addicts who want your money; in the evenings the general rule is not to enter the park unless there are other people about – if you do, stick to well-illuminated areas.

View of the city from Casa de Campo

ATTRACTIONS FOR CHILDREN

See Top 25 Sights for
PARQUE DEL OESTE (▶25)
PARQUE DEL RETIRO (▶46)

Tren de la Fresa

This old steam train, on which hostesses in costume serve strawberries to passengers, is called the Strawberry Train because it runs between Madrid and the strawberry fields of Aranjuez. A hundred years ago this was a favourite weekend jaunt for *madrileños*. Tickets can be booked from many travel agents, and include entrance to the Royal Palace and gardens in Aranjuez.

ACCIONA

Acciona is Madrid's first interactive science museum, 3,500sq m of floor space housing hands-on exhibits which teach children that science can be fun. Sections include 'Sailing through Images' and 'A World of Molecules', but all in Spanish. There is a special room for smaller children. Acciona's main disadvantage is its distance from the centre.

✉ Pintor Murillo. Parque de Andalucía, Alcobendas ☎ 661 39 09 ⏰ Mon–Fri 10–6; Sat, Sun and public hols 10–8 🚇 Plaza Castilla (for bus departures) 🚌 Plaza Castilla (every 20 minutes)

AQUÓPOLIS

This is the one Spanish children beg their parents to take them to. Aquópolis is the biggest and best of the Madrid waterparks, and one of the largest in Europe, with huge water slides, an adventure lake and wave machines.

✉ Villanueva de la Cañada. Carretera de El Escorial 25km 🍴 ££

FARO DE MONCLOA

Located opposite the entrance to the Museo de América, this stainless steel tower was built in 1992 and is 92m high. It offers a panoramic view from the centre of Madrid.

➕ C7 ✉ Avenida de la Victoria ☎ 544 81 04 ⏰ Daily 10:30–1:45, 2:30–7:15 (8:15 in summer) 🚇 Moncloa 🚌 16, 61, 83, 84, 92, 93, 95 🎫 Cheap

PARQUE DE ATRACCIONES (CASA DE CAMPO)

This enormous fun-fair offers everything from old-style merry-go-rounds to the breathtaking Top Spin. There is also an open-air auditorium with concerts throughout the summer months; the fun carries on until way past bedtime.

➕ A9 ✉ Casa de Campo ☎ 463 64 33/463 29 00 ⏰ Daily noon–7; Sat and public hols noon–8 🍴 Cafés, restaurants 🚇 Batán 🚌 33, 36, 39, 65 🎫 Moderate

ZOO

Located in the Casa de Campo, Madrid's zoo is one of the best in Europe. It contains over 2,000 animals and more than 100 species of bird. Star of the show is Chulín, the giant panda. There is also a dolphinarium, with twice-daily shows, a train-ride, an aquarium and a special children's section.

➕ A9 ✉ Casa de Campo ☎ 711 99 50 ⏰ Daily 10–7:30 🍴 Cafés, restaurants 🚇 Batán 🚌 33, Ventas – Zoo, Batán – Zoo, Estrecho – Zoo, Peñaprieta – Zoo 🎫 Expensive

The dolphinarium – a perennial attraction at the zoo in the Casa de Campo

INTERESTING STREETS

ARENAL
Connecting Sol with Opera, the Calle Arenal has a 19th-century air. During the Middle Ages it was no more than a ravine, but after 1656 it began to compete with the Calle Mayor in importance, perhaps because it was the shortest route between the Royal Palace and Sol. Highlights are the San Ginés Church and the Joy Esclava discotheque.
⊞ bII, D9 🚇 Sol, Opera 🚌 5, 15, 20, 51, 52, 53, 150

GRAN VÍA
Running between the Calle Alcalá and the Plaza de España, the overbearing Gran Vía is one of the city's great axes; with its shops and cinemas it is a lively and stimulating place for an early evening stroll. Begun in 1910 under Alfonso XII, its construction led to the shortening or destruction of 54 other streets. Highlights are the Grassy Reloj and Telefónica buildings.
⊞ bcdI, DE8 🚇 Gran Vía, Callao 🚌 44, 46, 74, 133, 146, 147, 148, 149

MAYOR
This is perhaps the most 'traditional' of Madrid's streets, and the peculiarly *madrileño* nature of the shops – including a rather wonderful *guitarrería* near the Calle Bailén end – are instances of this. The street also has literary associations: Spain's two greatest playwrights, Lope de Vega and Calderón de la Barca, lived at Nos. 25 and 61 respectively.
⊞ abII, D9 🚇 Sol 🚌 3

MESÓN DE PAREDES
For the full, slightly surreal atmosphere of Madrid's *barrio popular*, a stroll down this street and those around it on any weekday morning cannot be bettered. La Corrala, an open-air theatre, no longer functions as such; it was restored in 1979 and has now been declared an Artistic Monument.
⊞ bcIII–IV, D9–10 🚇 Tirso de Molina, Lavapiés 🚌 32, 57

PASEO DE LA CASTELLANA
Running in an almost straight line from Colón in the centre to Plaza de Castilla in the north – a distance of some 6km – the Castellana is one of Madrid's main points of reference. It splits the city in two, with many of the major sights located on or around it.
⊞ E2–8 🚇 Colón, Rubén Darío, Nuevos Ministerios, Lima, Cuzco, Plaza de Castilla 🚌 5, 14, 27, 40, 45, 147, 149, 150

Streets and sky
A walk round the streets of any of Madrid's *barrios* is a quick and easy way of defining the flavour of that part of the city. *Madrileños* live on the streets, particularly during the summer, thus any description of the streets is also a portrait of the people who work and live there. Be careful to look upwards, too: on a clear day, the contrast between the buildings and the blue sky is exhilarating.

The Gran Vía, one of Madrid's major streets

59

CURIOSITIES

ARAB WALL
What little we can see of the *muralla Árabe* is the oldest surviving part of Madrid. It was originally part of the walls of the small Arab town of Magerit. The area around it is now called the Parque Emir Mohammed I, and is one of the venues for Madrid's autumn arts festival.

➕ all, C9 ✉ Cuesta de la Vega Ⓜ Opera 🚌 3, 41, 148

ATOCHA RAILWAY STATION
The architecture combines the impressive, late 18th-century wrought-iron and glass architecture of Alberto del Palacio with a 2,000sq m indoor tropical garden.

➕ dIV, E10 ✉ Plaza del Emperador Carlos V ☎ 527 31 60 Ⓜ Atocha Renfe, Atocha 🚌 14, 27, 34, 37, 45 ♿ Few

Façade of the Atocha Railway Station

HOUSE OF SEVEN CHIMNEYS
Legend has it that Philip II built it for one of his mistresses, who is supposed to haunt the house. When restoration work was done a while ago, the skeleton of a woman was discovered, with some coins from the period of Philip II near by.

➕ dI, E8 ✉ Plaza del Rey Ⓜ Banco de España 🚌 1, 2, 74, 146

SALA DEL CANAL DE ISABEL II
Considered one of Madrid's finest examples of industrial architecture, this display space, built in neo-Mudéjar style between 1907 and 1911, is particularly strong on photographic exhibitions.

➕ D6 ✉ Calle Santa Engracia 125 ☎ 445 10 00 🕐 Daily Tue–Sat 10–2, 5–9; Sun and public hols 10–2. Closed Mon Ⓜ Cuatro Caminos 🚌 3, 37, 149 🎫 Free

TORRES KIO (PUERTA DE EUROPA)
These Towers at the Castellana in Plaza de Castilla are named after the Kuwaiti Investment Office who withdrew funding half-way through their construction. A symbol of the decline of the economic boom, they are angled inwards at 15°, the architectural maximum short of collapse.

➕ E3 ✉ Plaza de Castilla Ⓜ Plaza de Castilla 🚌 5, 27, 42, 124, 125, 147, 149

VIADUCT
Otherwise known as 'the Suicide Bridge', for reasons which become obvious as you stand looking down on the Calle de Segovia far below.

➕ C9 ✉ Calle Bailén Ⓜ Opera 🚌 3, 148

Curious facts about Madrid
Like any big city, Madrid has its fair share of the simply odd. There is, for example, no No. 13 bus route, and the 13th floor of the Torre Picasso is occupied by an unlucky-for-some insurance agency. Another curious fact is that Madrid has not been particularly careful about the remains of some of its greatest artists: the whereabouts of Velázquez, Lope de Vega and Cervantes are unknown, while the skeleton of Goya is headless.

TAVERNA

MADRID
where to...

EXPENSIVE RESTAURANTS

Prices
In a luxury restaurant expect to pay 7,500–12,000ptas, including wine.

Tips
Many of Madrid's better restaurants are less enjoyable at lunchtime, when they attract a mainly business clientele, than in the evenings. Only Zalacaín insists on a jacket and tie. The pricier restaurants are the only places where there is a chance that the waiter will speak English.

CABO MAYOR
A Madrid classic, specialising in dishes based on the cuisine of Cantabria in northern Spain. Elegant nautically inspired décor, and a relaxed atmosphere. The lobster salad and the desserts are particularly good.
✚ F4 ✉ Calle Juan Ramón Jiménez 37 ☎ 350 87 76 🕐 Closed Easter week and Aug 🚇 Plaza de Castilla, Cuzco

CLUB 31
One of Madrid's finest restaurants serving international dishes with a bias on game. Particularly good is the partridge with grapes. Formal and elegant, with impeccable service.
✚ E8 ✉ Calle Alcalá 58 ☎ 531 00 92 🕐 Closed Aug 🚇 Retiro

EL AMPARO
Lovingly designed with an eye on tradition and constructed around a small interior patio area, El Amparo's cuisine is based on Basque dishes. The wine list runs to more than 500 different wines.
✚ F8 ✉ Callejón de Puigcerdá 8 ☎ 431 64 56 🕐 Closed Aug 🚇 Serrano

HORCHER
Horcher is perhaps the best-known restaurant in Madrid after Zalacaín. Established in 1943 and family-run, it bases its exquisite menu on central European dishes and game.
✚ E9 ✉ Calle Alfonso XII 6 ☎ 522 07 31 🕐 Closed Aug 🚇 Retiro

JOCKEY
Designed with an intimate British feel, Jockey was recently voted the best restaurant in Madrid. The sea-urchin omelette is one of the more daring choices.
✚ E8 ✉ Amador de los Rios 6 ☎ 319 24 35 🚇 Colón

PRÍNCIPE DE VIANA
Owned by the same family as the legendary Zalacaín: haute cuisine based on the Basque/Navarre region. Has recently brought its prices down, but the menu remains the same.
✚ F4 ✉ Manuel de Falla 5 ☎ 457 15 49 🚇 Lima, Cuzco

VIRIDIANA
The décor here consists principally of stills from Buñuel movies. An extremely creative menu, and a more laid-back atmosphere than many of the better restaurants.
✚ dII, E9 ✉ Calle Juan de Mena 14 ☎ 523 44 78 🕐 Closed Aug 🚇 Retiro

ZALACAÍN
Generally considered one of the best restaurants in Madrid (the only one with three Michelin stars) and one of the best in Spain. The menu, based on Basque/Navarre cuisine, changes according to season and the whims of the head chef, Benjamín Urdiain.
✚ E6 ✉ Alvarez de Baena 4 ☎ 561 48 40 🕐 Closed Christmas and Easter week 🚇 Rubén Darío

MID-PRICE RESTAURANTS

BOTÍN

Madrid's oldest restaurant, which makes it extremely popular with visitors. Three floors, with ornamental tiling and a wood-fired oven, offering traditional Castilian roasts.

bI, D9 ⊠ Calle Cuchilleros 17 ☎ 366 42 17 ⓜ Sol

CASA CIRIACO

At the bottom of Plaza Mayor, Casa Ciriaco offers traditional Madrid cuisine in a pleasantly unfussy environment which Madrid celebrities seem to like. The chicken in a wine and garlic sauce (*pepitoria de gallina*) is legendary.

aII, D9 ⊠ Calle Mayor 84 ☎ 548 06 20 ⓒ Closed Aug ⓜ Opera

CASA LUCIO

A classic of Madrid, to which the King has been known to bring visitors. The least touristy of the traditional restaurants, Casa Lucio specialises in Castilian roasts, but offers several Basque dishes too.

aIII, D9 ⊠ Cava Baja 35 ☎ 365 32 52 ⓒ Closed Aug ⓜ La Latina, Tirso de Molina

CASA PACO

Its red façade, the bullfighting décor, the old oak bar and its location make Casa Paco popular with visitors and locals alike. The food (including ten different kinds of *tortilla*) is probably the best in this price range.

bIII, D9 ⊠ Puerta Cerrada 11 ☎ 366 31 66 ⓒ Closed Aug ⓜ Tirso de Molina

EL BUEY

Slivers of ox meat are served raw and then cooked to taste on red-hot plates by the customers themselves. The original El Buey is at Calle General Pandiñas 10 (☎ 431 44 92), but this is the more pleasantly located. An excellent range of Ribera de Duero wines.

aI, C8 ⊠ Plaza de la Marina Española ☎ 541 30 41 ⓜ Santo Domingo

EL LAR DEL BUEY

Combining the rustic and the elegant with open brickwork and a vaulted ceiling, El Lar del Buey serves charcoal-roasted ox meat and delicious desserts.

dI, E8 ⊠ Calle Almirante 11 ☎ 531 14 94 ⓒ Closed first two weeks of Aug ⓜ Chueca, Colón

LA DORADA

Opened in 1980 along the lines of owner Félix Cabezas' Seville restaurant, La Dorada has a distinctly nautical flavour, with separate 'cabins' for intimacy. The cuisine is Andalucian, based around seafood and fish.

E4 ⊠ Calle Orense 64–66 ☎ 570 20 04 ⓒ Closed Aug ⓜ Tetuán

Prices

In a moderately priced restaurant expect to pay 4,000–7,500ptas, including wine.

El menu del día

By law, Spanish restaurants have to offer a fixed-price menu with a range of first and second courses, a dessert and a drink. These are advertised outside the restaurant. How much this costs depends on the restaurant, but you will find a perfectly good example of home cooking for somewhere in the 900–1,200ptas range. Coffee is either extra or an alternative to the dessert.

Budget Restaurants

Prices

In a budget restaurant expect to pay 1,500–4,000ptas, including wine.

Fast food

Like every other city, Madrid has been invaded by takeaway services – best avoided if possible, but sometimes a necessary evil. The following telephone numbers might not serve your neighbourhood, but if a service exists in your area, they will supply you with the number you need. Tele-Burger (hamburgers, etc): 533 65 14; Telepaella (paella): 459 20 10; Telepescaito (seafood): 767 05 13; Teleservice (Chinese): 401 44 78; Teletortilla (tortilla): 725 52 03.

ALBUR

Excellent Spanish 'home cooking' with a different menu every day, all based on typical regional dishes. Very reasonably priced.
➕ D7 ✉ Calle Manuela Malasaña ☎ 594 27 33
🚇 Bilbao

ARTEMISA

One of very few vegetarian restaurants, and generally considered to be the best. Green beans in a pine-nut and mayonnaise sauce is a speciality.
➕ cII, E9 ✉ Ventura de la Vega 4 ☎ 429 50 92 🚇 Sol

EL ALBA

This cheap, very friendly restaurant in the *barrio popular* is crowded out at weekends. The waiters are a good double act; one of them supports Real Madrid, the other Atlético.
➕ bIII, D9 ✉ Plaza Duque de Alba 2 ☎ 365 2540 🚇 Tirso de Molina

HYLOGUI

Enormous and generally bustling, Hylogui is one of the better 'home cooking' establishments, with more than 100 items on the menu, and better-than-average service. There are generally queues at weekends.
➕ cII, E9 ✉ Calle Ventura de la Vega 3 ☎ 429 73 57
🕐 Closed Aug 🚇 Sevilla

SALVADOR

The standard clientele at Salvador is an interesting mixture of intellectuals and bullfighters, in the spirit of one of its best clients, Ernest Hemingway. Traditional food, with oxtail and cod fritters amongst the dishes.
➕ dI, E8 ✉ Calle Barbieri 12 ☎ 521 45 24 🕐 Closed Aug 🚇 Chueca, Gran Vía

SAMARKANDA

A colonial-style restaurant set in the 'tropical garden' section of the Atocha railway station, Samarkanda does more than just cash in on its location. If you can, get table No. 20. Light, modern cuisine.
➕ E10 ✉ Glorieta de Carlos V, Atocha Railway Station ☎ 530 97 46 🚇 Atocha

TIENDA DE VINOS

Basic food of variable quality, but with lots of history and atmosphere, the Tienda de Vinos was a Communist gathering-place under the old Franco regime. The service, though, does not come with a smile.
➕ cI, D8 ✉ Calle Augusto Figueroa 35 ☎ 521 70 12 🚇 Chueca

VIUDA DE VACAS

Traditional Spanish home cooking amidst the typical *azulejo* tiles, spiral staircase and wooden tables of old Madrid. This is one place where the *madrileños* like to bring their overseas visitors. Excellent value.
➕ bIII, D9 ✉ Calle Cava Alta 33 ☎ 366 58 47 🕐 Closed Aug 🚇 La Latina

BEST REGIONAL RESTAURANTS

MADRILEÑO/GALICIAN

CASA DOMINGO (£)
Callos (tripe) is the speciality in this 1920s decorated, somewhat noisy restaurant, which spills out on to the pavement opposite the Parque del Retiro in summer. *Tortilla de bacalao* (cod tortilla) is another local speciality. Wonderful home-made desserts.

✚ F8 ✉ Calle Alcalá 99 ☎ 576 01 37 🚇 Retiro

CASA GALLEGA (£)
Specialises in largely fish-based Galician cuisine, but also serves fabulous Padrón peppers, and there are wonderful *tapas* in the basement bar. Friendly, but a little slow. There is another branch at Calle Bordadores 11 ☎ 541 90 55.

✚ bII, D9 ✉ Plaza de San Miguel 8 ☎ 547 30 55 🚇 Sol

HOGAR GALLEGO (££)
Just off the Plaza Mayor and with outdoor seating in summer, the 'Galician Home' is the most popular Galician restaurant with visitors owing to its location.

✚ bII, D9 ✉ Plaza Comandante Morenas 3 ☎ 542 48 26 🕐 Closed Aug 🚇 Sol

LA BOLA (£)
The *cocido* (see side panel), which is La Bola's speciality, is still prepared as it has been since the last century, in large earthenware pots over a wood fire. Popular with visitors for its traditional feel; reservation is advisable.

✚ aI, D8 ✉ Calle Bola 5 ☎ 547 6930 🕐 Closed Jul and Aug 🚇 Santo Domingo

LA FREIDURÍA DE GALLINEJAS (£)
Fry-shops like this were once very popular. Typical Madrid cuisine at its most hardcore. Offal of lamb and stomach linings without trimmings are yours at a very low price, as well as *criadillos* (bull's testicles), more often talked about than eaten.

✚ D10 ✉ Calle Embajadores 84 ☎ 517 59 33 🚇 Embajadores

O'PAZO (£££)
A marvellous range of typical Galician dishes from this restaurant owned by the king of Galician cuisine in Madrid, Don Evaristo García Gómez. Seafood cocktail, Aguinaga eels, mussels and the classic Galician dessert, *tarta de Santiago*, are amongst the most-requested items.

✚ E5 ✉ Calle Reina Mercedes 20 ☎ 553 23 33 🕐 Closed Easter week and Aug 🚇 Estrecho

TABERNA LA DANIELA (£)
Attractive *azulejo* (tiled) décor, but this time with a modern feel. *Cocido* is the speciality, but they also serve another typically *madrileño* dish, *besugo a la madrileña* (red bream), which must be ordered in advance.

✚ F8 ✉ Calle General Pardiñas 21 ☎ 575 23 29 🕐 Closed Aug 🚇 Goya, Nuñez de Balboa

Prices

£ = 1,500–4,000ptas

££ = 4,000–7,500ptas

£££ = 7,500–12,000ptas

Madrid gastronomy

The preferred food of *los madrileños* is based around those animal parts which tend to produce a grimace of disgust – offal (the spicy *callos a la madrileña*), pig's ears (*orejas*), brains (*sesos*) and the different kinds of blood sausage, or *morcilla*. The classic *cocido completo* is perhaps the most acceptable dish to the non-native palate: first a noodle soup, then a main course with chickpeas and other vegetables and meat, all of which have been cooked together.

BEST REGIONAL RESTAURANTS

CATALAN/VALENCIAN/BASQUE/ASTURIAN

A restaurant guide

Spanish regional cuisine – particularly that of the Basque country – has achieved greater international recognition than the cuisine of Madrid itself. There are many restaurants in Madrid: several guides are available, but the best is *En Boca de Todos*, updated annually, which gathers together the opinions of *los madrileños* themselves as to the best – and the not-so-good.

AL-MANZOR (£)

Located in the La Mezquita or Mosque cultural centre, Al-Manzor offers reasonably priced Arab cuisine in fascinating surroundings. Since you have to cross the mosque to get to the restaurant, women are lent a tunic to cover their legs.
✚ H7 ⊠ Salvador de Madariaga 4 ☎ 326 64 63 🕔 During Ramadan open 4–midnight 🚇 El Carmen

AL-MOUNIA (££)

Moroccan cuisine in a restaurant with beautifully detailed Arab-style décor. Though not particularly cheap, Al-Mounia serves Madrid's best North African cuisine, with kebabs and a delicious lamb couscous.
✚ dI, E8 ⊠ Calle Recoletos 5 ☎ 435 08 28 🕔 Closed Aug 🚇 Banco de España

CAN PUNYETES (£)

Typical Catalan cuisine (including *butifarra* sausage, grilled meats, patés and cheeses) in an environment redolent of former times.
✚ aII, D9 ⊠ Calle Señores de Luzón 5 ☎ 542 09 21 🚇 Sol

CASA PORTAL (££)

Asturian cuisine is highly prized in Spain, and Casa Portal – with its walls of sacking, homely atmosphere, and a menu including *fabada* (bean stew) and hake in cider – is a good place to try it.
✚ F8 ⊠ Calle Doctor Casteló 26 ☎ 574 20 26 🕔 Closed Aug 🚇 Retiro

DE FUNY (£)

A limited but well-prepared range of Lebanese cuisine, with the hake in sesame sauce particularly good. There is also a belly-dancer. Best visited at weekends, when the atmosphere is liveliest.
✚ F5 ⊠ Calle Serrano 213 ☎ 457 69 15 🚇 Colombia

ENDAVANT (££)

Spacious, with a Mediterranean air and Catalan-based cuisine including snails and a delicious *crema catalana* (custard). Also has a garden/terrace during the summer.
✚ F6 ⊠ Calle Velázquez 160 ☎ 561 27 38 🚇 República Argentina

EL CENTRO CUBANO (£)

The Cuban Centre is as much a cultural project as a restaurant: the walls are covered with press-cuttings and photos of Cuban stars past and present. Very reasonably priced, with *ropa vieja* (meat stew) and *arroz a la cubana* (rice with tomato sauce and a banana) among the items on the menu.
✚ F8 ⊠ Calle Claudio Coello ☎ 577 84 01 🚇 Serrano

EL CHALET (£)

Argentinian cuisine, prepared in front of the customers. Not very intimate, but quite lively, particularly at weekends, and with a pleasant terrace. There is another branch at Arturo Soria 207 ☎ 415 64 00.

🞡 G5 ✉ Alfonso XIII 39 ☎ 413 13 23 🞄 Closed Aug 🞄 Alfonso XIII

EL INTI DE ORO (£)

Start your meal here with a typically Peruvian *pisco* cocktail. A pleasant, intimate environment, attentive service and a generally young clientele. Very reasonably priced.

🞡 dII, E9 ✉ Calle Ventura de la Vega 12 ☎ 429 67 03 🞄 Sol

ENTRE SUSPIRO Y SUSPIRO (££)

The best Mexican restaurant in Madrid in food terms, but not large, so it is best to book ahead. Very colourful, with a menu in verse.

🞡 aI, C8 ✉ Plaza de la Marina Española 4 ☎ 542 06 44 🞄 Closed Aug 🞄 Santo Domingo

GAZTELUPE (££)

Considered to be one of Madrid's finest restaurants (though reasonably priced), Gaztelupe serves beautifully prepared Basque cuisine – meat and fish cooked in a wide variety of different ways. Pre-booking is advisable.

🞡 E5 ✉ Calle Comandante

Zorita 32 ☎ 534 90 28 🞄 Estrecho, Nuevos Ministerios

GURI-ETXEA (££)

Built on the site of an 18th-century wine cellar in the old part of town, Guri-Etxea is considered by many to serve the best traditional Basque dishes in Madrid. Has a wide range of Basque Txacoli wines.

🞡 aIII, C9 ✉ Plaza de la Paja 12 ☎ 365 61 49 🞄 Closed Aug 🞄 La Latina

LA BARRACA (££)

Rice is at the heart of Valencian cuisine. La Barraca has 16 different varieties on the menu, the best of which is the house *paella*. Prettily decorated with Valencian plates and porcelain.

🞡 dI, D8 ✉ Calle Reina 29 ☎ 532 71 54 🞄 Gran Via

LA TAQUERÍA (£)

An atmospheric Mexican bar/restaurant. There is another branch in Plaza Comendadoras 2 ☎ 522 80 49. *Tacos del pastor*, prepared in the traditional way, *enchiladas* and, of course, wonderful *margaritas*.

🞡 aIII, C9 ✉ Calle Don Pedro 11 ☎ 365 10 77 🞄 La Latina

New tastes

Both Latin American and North African cuisine – for historical and geographical reasons – are increasingly gaining footholds in Madrid's hitherto fairly conservative culinary scene. The menus in these places can be as incomprehensible to Spaniards as to any visitor. The best bet is to see what others are eating and base your choice on that.

COFFEE, TEA & CHOCOLATE

La tertulia

Madrid's *tertulia* (literary gathering) culture is largely a thing of the past. Until not so long ago writers, philosophers and artists would meet to drink coffee, smoke and debate ideas, causing poet and musician Emilio Cerrère to declare that 'it is well known that most literary masterpieces have been written in cafés'. The *tertulia* also gave rise to another phenomenon: the so-called *naufragos del café* or 'coffee shipwrecks', those men who went to *tertulias* only to become lost in a world of unrealisable dreams.

CAFÉ COMERCIAL
'Time hasn't actually stopped in this café,' declared the newspaper *El País*, 'but it does move imperceptibly slowly.' The Comercial, calm through the day but hectic at night, has long been Madrid's best-known meeting-point.
✚ D7 ✉ Glorieta de Bilbao 7 ☎ 521 56 55 🕓 Closed Aug Ⓜ Bilbao

CAFÉ DEL BOTÁNICO
Its position next to the Prado and the Retiro makes this one of the better-located cafés, and it has a *terraza* area during the summer.
✚ E9 ✉ Calle Ruiz de Alarcón 27 ☎ 420 23 42 Ⓜ Atocha, Banco de España

CAFÉ DEL NUNCIO
The Nuncio is at its best during the summer, when a *terraza* is set up. A friendly place in the heart of the old quarter.
✚ aIII, D9 ✉ Calle Segovia 9 ☎ 366 09 06 Ⓜ La Latina

CAFÉ DE ORIENTE
Sumptuous décor and a good view of the Palacio Real have won the Oriente a reputation for being one of the more exclusive cafés.
✚ aII, C9 ✉ Plaza de Oriente 2 ☎ 547 15 64 Ⓜ Opera

CAFÉ GIJÓN
The Gijón is best known for its literary associations (see side panel). These have faded with the years, but the Gijón is still a pleasant place to stop.
✚ dI, E8 ✉ Paseo de Recoletos 21 ☎ 521 54 25 Ⓜ Banco de España, Colón

CAFÉ RUIZ
A relatively peaceful retreat from the night-time mayhem of the surrounding *barrio* of Malasaña, the Ruiz retains a late 19th-century feel and serves cocktails as well as coffee and milkshakes.
✚ D7 ✉ Calle Ruiz 11 ☎ 446 12 32 Ⓜ Bilbao

EL ESPEJO
With fabulous art-nouveau décor and a terrace, El Espejo looks more expensive than it is.
✚ dI, E8 ✉ Paseo de Recoletos 31 ☎ 308 23 47 Ⓜ Colón

EMBASSY
Madrid is short on tea-rooms, but this is the best, serving a wide range of teas as well as chocolates, cakes, sandwiches and scones.
✚ E8 ✉ Paseo de la Castellana 12 ☎ 576 00 80 Ⓜ Colón

NUEVO CAFÉ BARBIERI
Has a columned interior and attracts a young clientele.
✚ dIV, D10 ✉ Calle Avemaría 45 ☎ 527 36 58 Ⓜ Lavapiés

CHOCOLATERÍA SAN GINÉS
Three minutes from Sol. Flashy, big, extremely busy, especially during the winter months. Burnt down in 1993, but has now reopened.
✚ bII, D9 ✉ Pasaje de San Ginés 5 ☎ 365 65 46 Ⓜ Sol/Opera

TAPAS

CASA HUMANES

Casa Humanes was popular with the likes of King Alfonso XII. With its well-preserved 1897 décor, and location in the heart of the traditional neighbourhood, it maintains the habit of selling tiny glasses of red wine at 25ptas a shot. Displays its *tapas*.

✚ D10 ✉ Calle Embajadores 80 🕐 Closed Aug 🚇 Embajadores

CASA LABRA

This is where the Spanish Socialist Party was founded in 1879. Itself founded in 1860, Casa Labra has been producing typically *madrileño tapas* ever since, with cod croquettes a speciality.

✚ cII, D9 ✉ Calle Tetuán 12 ☎ 531 00 81 🚇 Sol

CASA MINGO

A popular Asturian *sidrería* or cider house: the tradition is to pour the cider into the glass from a great height and drink it very fast. The best *tapas* are those based on the strong *Cabrales* cheese. Also an excellent restaurant.

✚ B8 ✉ Paseo de la Florida 2 ☎ 547 79 18 🚇 Norte

EL ANCIANO REY DE LOS VINOS

Particularly famous for its wines, this is one of the more historic taverns of Madrid, with tiled *azulejo* décor adding to the effect. Typically Madrid *tapas* are available, such as fried cod, tripe and meatballs.

✚ cII, D9 ✉ Calle de la Paz ☎ 532 14 73 🕐 Closed Aug 🚇 Sol

JOSÉ LUIS

Located firmly at the non-traditional end of the *tapas* bars, José Luis offers a wide range of 'international-based' *tapas*, such as smoked salmon tartare and melted brie.

✚ F7 ✉ Calle Serrano 89 ☎ 563 09 58 🚇 Serrano

LHARDY

As well as being one of the classier restaurants in the city and a local institution, Lhardy offers a good range of (fairly pricey) *tapas*, including consommé (to which you help yourself) croquettes, Russian salad on bread and, in summer, Madrid's best gazpacho. Displays its *tapas*.

✚ cII, D9 ✉ Calle Carrera de San Jerónimo 8 ☎ 522 22 07 🚇 Sol

TABERNA DE ANTONIO SÁNCHEZ

The best-conserved of all the *tapas* bars, as well as a homage to the bullfighting family which has run it since 1830. Interesting memorabilia (including bulls' heads) make Antonio Sánchez as fascinating for its atmosphere as for its *tapas*.

✚ bIII, D9 ✉ Calle Mesón de Paredes 13 ☎ 539 78 26/62 68 🚇 Tirso de Molina

Tapas

The *tapa*, or snack to accompany your drink, is a part of Spanish culture: it started in the 18th century when Carlos III insisted that his entourage cover their wine with a plate of food to stop dust getting into it (*tapa* means 'lid'). Giving *tapas* away free with a drink is largely a thing of the past, and many bars no longer display their wares, which can make ordering a complicated business. Expect to pay for what you have eaten and drunk before leaving, rather than on a round-by-round basis.

BEST SHOPS & SHOPPING MALLS

For better or worse, the retail scene in Madrid is becoming increasingly dominated by the chain stores or *centros comerciales* (shopping malls). But it is important, too, to try and get into the back streets, visit some of the smaller establishments, and join the queue: perhaps it is there that the atmosphere of Madrid is best enjoyed. The larger stores are open through lunch, while most of the smaller ones continue, in time-honoured fashion, to close from about 1:30 to about 4:30.

CENTRO COMERCIAL MADRID-2, LA VAGUADA

Madrid's largest and brashest commercial centre, with over 300 stores. The floor devoted to leisure pursuits includes a cinema, discotheque and bars.
✚ D2 ✉ Monforte de Lemos 36 ☎ 730 10 00 Ⓜ Barrio del Pilar

CITYVIPS/VIPS

The 12 bright and bold VIPS stores dotted around the city suffer a little in quality from trying to do everything – they sell books, magazines and records, food and gifts as well as offering a bar and restaurant – but they are an impressive size and convenient.
✚ bI, D8 ✉ Gran Vía 43 (with branches throughout the city) ☎ 559 64 57 Ⓜ Callao

EL CORTE INGLÉS

The English Cut totally dominates the Spanish retail market. It is possible to buy more or less anything at one of these multi-storey department stores, of which there are four in Madrid. They are so vast it is almost absurd, offering services as well as goods and a well-stocked supermarket. There is an information desk, staffed by multi-lingual assistants.
✚ F8 ✉ Calle Goya 76 (with branches at Calle Preciados 3; Calle Princesa 42; Raimundo Fernández Villaverde 79) ☎ 556 23 00 Ⓜ Goya

EL JARDÍN DE SERRANO

A small and elegant cluster of fashion and accessory stores, the Serrano Garden is in the heart of Madrid's most fashionable area, the *barrio Salamanca*.
✚ F8 ✉ Calle Goya 6–8 ☎ 577 04 06 Ⓜ Serrano

FNAC

An idea imported from France, this complex offers five floors of books and CDs. There is also a small concert area where you can occasionally hear big names, and an efficient concert-booking service.
✚ bI, D8 ✉ Calle Preciados 28 ☎ 595 62 00 Ⓜ Callao

GALERÍA DEL PRADO

Situated in the basement of the Palace Hotel, this small, well-organised mall offers 39 stores mainly devoted to fashion, a seating area in which to have a drink, and an all-day restaurant.
✚ dII, E9 ✉ Plaza de las Cortes 7 ☎ 420 08 78 Ⓜ Atocha

NEWSPAPER KIOSK IN PUERTA DEL SOL

This is the only one of the city's hundreds of bright, cheerful kiosks which is open 24 hours a day. It sells not only foreign newspapers and a startling range of pornography, but also academic studies of Nietzsche and Kant.
✚ bII, D9 ✉ Puerta del Sol Ⓜ Sol

TRENDIEST SHOPS

ADOLFO DOMÍNGUEZ
The work of Spain's best-known fashion designer is characterised by its beautiful, classic cut and its subdued colours. There is a men's shop close by, at Calle Ortega y Gasset 4.
✚ F6 ✉ Calle Serrano 96 ☎ 576 70 53 🚇 Rubén Darío

AGATHA RUIZ DE LA PRADA
Agatha's daring, brightly coloured patchwork-based designs still fly the flag for the *movida*, that long-gone time in the mid-1980s when Madrid believed everything was there just to be enjoyed. Every Thursday at 8PM, the public are invited in to have a drink and see what is happening.
✚ E7 ✉ Calle Marques de Riscal 8 ☎ 310 44 83 🚇 Rubén Darío

ÁLVAREZ-GÓMEZ
With more than 100 years in the perfume business, this is a Madrid classic. Also manufactures its own in-house cologne.
✚ E8 ✉ Calle Serrano 14 ☎ 431 16 56 🚇 Serrano

ARMANI
Elegance, simplicity and high prices are what Armani is famous for. The sobriety and elegance of its décor provides the best possible showcase for the clothes. There is a slightly cheaper Emporio Armani at Claudio Coello 77.
✚ F7 ✉ Calle Serrano 68 ☎ 576 10 36 🚇 Nuñez de Balboa

EKSEPTION
Ekseption succeeds in living up to its mis-spelt name, its spectacular 900sq m of floor space carrying rebellious designs from the likes of Jean Paul Gaultier, Dolce and Gabanna, and Vivienne Westwood.
✚ F8 ✉ Calle Velázquez 28 ☎ 577 14 60 🚇 Velázquez

ESCADA
The fashion designs of Marghareta Ley's German house blend bright colours in distinctive, unconventional ways.
✚ F7 ✉ Calle Ortega y Gasset 21 ☎ 577 41 88 🚇 Nuñez de Balboa

FARRUTX
Has an international reputation for its shoes, combining the finest quality leather with a wide range of in-house designs to suit all tastes.
✚ E8 ✉ Calle Serrano 7 ☎ 576 94 93 🚇 Serrano

LOEWE
This is the Spanish design firm with the greatest prestige abroad, and best known for its leather bags and fashion accessories.
✚ E8 ✉ Calle Serrano 26 ☎ 577 60 56 🚇 Serrano

ROBERTO VERINO
Verino's reputation both in Spain and abroad is steadily increasing, and his designs with their simple, elegant lines are a joy.
✚ F8 ✉ Calle Claudio Coello 27 ☎ 577 73 81 🚇 Serrano

Madrid fashion
Though not yet Paris, Rome, London or even Barcelona, Madrid is slowly gaining a foothold in the world of men's and women's fashion. The international success of Adolfo Domínguez has been followed by that of Roberto Verino, and together with the avant-garde designs of Agatha Ruiz de la Prada and Jesús del Pozo, the Spanish-based designers are proving a serious threat to the more established Italians. The *beau monde* does much of its shopping in the *barrio* Salamanca.

MARKETS & SHOPPING STREETS

The municipal food markets

There are many of these dotted around Madrid. Each *barrio* has its own, and they all offer a vast range of foodstuffs at extremely competitive prices, as well as a lot of atmosphere. Of them all, San Miguel (Plaza de San Miguel), because it is right in the centre of town, Maravillas (Bravo Murillo, 122), because it is the biggest, and Chamartín (Calle Potosí), because it is the most elegantly laid out, are most worth a visit. There are housewives in these places who would kill to save a few pesetas on a clove of garlic.

CALLE ALMIRANTE

During the 1980s, the Calle Almirante became a kind of Calle de Carnaby. Although it has declined a little since then, it is still the best area Madrid has to offer away from the far less daring formality of Ortega y Gasset and Serrano.
⊞ E8 ⊠ Calle Almirante ⊚ Chueca

CALLE BARQUILLO

Barquillo is a collection of hi-fi shops which is second to none. Stiff competition means there is the odd bargain to be found.
⊞ dl, E8 ⊚ Chueca

CALLE JOSÉ ORTEGA Y GASSET

Now the most exclusive street, it offers such stores as Kenzo, Adolfo Domínguez and Giorgio Armani.
⊞ F/G7 ⊠ Calle José Ortega y Gasset ⊚ Rubén Darío, Nuñez de Balboa

CALLE DE LOS LIBREROS

For over a century this has been a second home for Madrid's bibliophiles, with particular emphasis on the academic. There is a wide range of second-hand books available.
⊞ bl, D8 ⊚ Santo Domingo

CALLE SERRANO

Along its length you will find Adolfo Domínguez, Loewe and GianFranco Ferré stores, though these days mixed in with good-quality chain stores.
⊞ F7, F8 ⊚ Serrano

CONDE DE BARAJAS MARKET

A pretty little square just behind the Plaza Mayor, where painters try to sell their latest masterpieces.
⊞ bll, D9 ⊠ Plaza del Conde de Barajas ⊚ Sunday morning ⊚ La Latina

MARQUÉS DE VIANA MARKET

Located in the *barrio* of Tetuán, this is traditionally an area of handicrafts experts.
⊞ D/E4 ⊠ Calle Marqués de Viana ⊚ Sunday morning ⊚ Tetuán

RASTRO STREET MARKET

On a Sunday morning, from about 10.30 to 3, the streets around Ribera de Curtidores are alive with people buying and selling just about everything. A lot of the wares, particularly in the side-streets, are no more than junk, but it is a great place for people-watching. Calle Ribera de Curtidores has furniture, antiques and camping shops.
⊞ blll/IV, D9/10 ⊠ Plaza de Cascorro, Calle Ribera and sidestreets ⊚ Sunday and public hols ⊚ La Latina, Tirso de Molina

STAMPS AND COINS MARKET

Under the archways of the Plaza Mayor, people meet to discuss the value of stamps and coins.
⊞ bll, D9 ⊠ Plaza Mayor ⊚ Sunday morning ⊚ Sol

ANTIQUE SHOPS

BARRIO SALAMANCA

This area of the city contains over 50 antique shops where the cost reflects the quality both of the products and the restoration work. There are nine shops in Calle Claudio Coello, six in Nuñez de Balboa and four in Calle Velázquez. Particularly worthy of note are Sant-Yago (Calle Hermosilla 37), specialising in glassware, the Mercadillo Balboa (Nuñez de Balboa 63), a collection of auction houses under one roof which sell as well as auction, the Almodena Escudero (Príncipe de Vergara 28), and La Trastienda de Alcalá (Calle Alcalá 64), specialising in high-quality reproductions.

✚ F8 ✉ *Barrio* Salamanca
Ⓜ Serrano, Velázquez, Nuñez de Balboa, Príncipe de Vergara

CALLE DEL PRADO

Fifteen antiques shops are concentrated in and around the Calle del Prado, which runs down from the Plaza de Santa Ana.

✚ cdll, DE9 ✉ Calle del Prado
Ⓜ Antón Martín

CENTRO DE ANTICUARIOS LAGASCA

Houses several different antiques stores, among which the most interesting are Lepina, Pedro Alarcón and Luis Carabe.

✚ F8 ✉ Calle Lagasca 36
Ⓜ Serrano

GALERIAS PIQUER

This pleasant shopping mall in the Rastro street market has 20 stores dedicated exclusively to the sale of antiques. Particularly worth a look are Hidalgo (old household objects), Siglo 20 (art deco), and El Estudio (Isabelline furniture and lamps).

✚ blll, D9 ✉ Calle Ribera de Curtidores 29 Ⓜ La Latina

GALERÍAS RIVERA

The smallest of the antiques malls in the Rastro street market, with just four shops.

✚ blll, D9 ✉ Ribera de Curtidores 15 Ⓜ La Latina

MERCADO PUERTA DE TOLEDO

Opened several years ago as a luxury shopping area, the Puerta de Toledo market has been an economic disaster, and its antique shops are always likely to close down. However, it is still worth a browse.

✚ alV, D10 ✉ Puerta de Toledo ☎ 366 45 03
Ⓜ Puerta de Toledo

NUEVAS GALERÍAS

The third antiques shopping mall in the Rastro street market, with 11 stores. Look for María Eugenia Falla (brass), González (bronze) and Sucesor de Cuenca (old office equipment). The attention to restoration detail is exemplary.

✚ blll, D9 ✉ Ribera de Curtidores 12 Ⓜ La Latina

Where to go

Madrid has a bewildering array of antique shops, but they are concentrated in three main areas: the *barrio* Salamanca, around the Calle del Prado and Santa Ana, and around the Rastro, particularly down the Calle Ribera de Curtidores. It is in the last that you are most likely to find a bargain.

BEST OFF-BEAT SHOPS

Lucky dip

The little specialist shops of Madrid can offer as much insight into the minds of its inhabitants as any museum. Sometimes, without a dictionary, it is hard to know what a shop is really selling. You would not actually want to buy anything at some of these places, but it is worth pausing to admire some of the more off-beat window displays, particularly in the area around the Plaza Mayor, La Latina and the area between Calle del Barco and Calle Hortaleza, just off the Gran Via. These have been lovingly put together by proprietors who know they are as much a part of the urban landscape as any monument.

CARAMELES PACO
Devoted exclusively to the sale of boiled sweets, Carameles Paco is a dentist's dream. There are sugary replicas – amongst other things – of elephants, rabbits and a village square, and the window display is unique.
🕀 bIII, D9 ✉ Calle Toledo 55 ☎ 365 42 58 🚇 La Latina

CORSETERÍA LA LATINA
Of the many women's underwear shops dotted around Madrid, this has perhaps the greatest reputation of them all – and the most sizzling window display, an awe-inspiring collection of outsized panty-girdles.
🕀 bIII, D9 ✉ Calle Toledo 49 ☎ 365 46 22 🚇 La Latina

FEKI
For 25 years, Feki have been making boxes of all sizes, shapes and colours. You can even have one made to order.
🕀 F8 ✉ Calle Hermosilla 56 ☎ 431 73 35 🚇 Velázquez

FILIGRANA
If it is 1960s music you want, this is the place – not only Anglo-American 1960s music, but Spanish and Latin-American too; wonderfully over-the-top stuff. One section is given over to the *copla*, Spain's version of the bodice-ripping ballad, while pride of place in the other section is occupied by a signed photo of Shirley Temple.
🕀 D8 ✉ Calle San Vicente Ferrer 28 ☎ 531 6357 🚇 Tribunal

JUSTO ALGABA
This is the place where bullfighters go. Though it specialises in 'suits of lights', there is also a wide range of other bullfighting paraphernalia on display.
🕀 cII, D9 ✉ Calle Paz 4 ☎ 523 35 95 🚇 Sol

LOS SIETE SOLES
Sells amulets and mythological statuettes for warding off bad luck. The AIDUN statuette, for example, helps you to find a job, while TRI is responsible for protecting married love.
🕀 bII, D9 ✉ Calle Mayor 73 ☎ 541 93 63 🚇 Sol/Opera

LUIS VILLASANTE
Specialising in material for religious habits, Luis Villasante gives saints' names to its various shades of cloth. Dark brown, for example, is 'Saint Francis of Assisi'. Also sells many other religious artefacts: the window display, full of models of Baby Jesus, is fascinating. There is similar fare at Sobrina Pérez, a little further along Calle Postas.
🕀 bII, D9 ✉ Calle Postas 14 ☎ 366 46 40 🚇 Sol

TIENDA ZIPPO
The only items sold here are Zippo cigarette lighters, 800 different models, ranging from 2,000ptas up to 40,000ptas for one in solid gold.
🕀 E5 ✉ Concha Espina 1, La Esquina del Bernabeu ☎ 344 16 40 🚇 Lima

FOOD & WINE SHOPS

BURGOS EL PALACIO DE LOS QUESOS

'The Cheese Palace' in Calle Mayor has had one of the capital's most mouth-watering window displays since 1919. The name says it all, really.

🕂 bII, D9 ✉ Calle Mayor 53 ☎ 548 16 23 🚇 Sol

CAFÉS POZO

This, the original of Madrid's three Cafés Pozo stores, has a wide range of coffees blended to order.

🕂 cIII, D9 ✉ Calle Magdalena 23 ☎ 369 07 64 🚇 Antón Martín

CASA LARREINA

Really a wine supermarket, Casa Larreina offers probably the widest range of wines in Madrid. This includes *all* the Spanish wines as well as a healthy foreign selection, and at a cheaper price than in many shops. There is another branch at Calle Francisco de Rojas 1.

🕂 F7 ✉ Calle Padilla 42 ☎ 577 62 73 🚇 Nuñez de Balboa

LA MALLORQUINA

Madrid's most central pastry shop greets people emerging from the Sol metro with the same delicious aroma it has had for years. The custard-filled *napolitanas*, still hot from the oven, are a treat.

🕂 cII, D9 ✉ Puerta del Sol 8 ☎ 521 12 01 🚇 Sol

MARIANO MADRUEÑO

Founded in 1895, this is one of the city's more traditional wine-shops or *bodegas*, with reasonable prices and still with the original wrought-iron, carved-wood décor.

🕂 bII, D8 ✉ Postigo de San Martín 3 ☎ 521 19 55 🚇 Callao

MÉNDEZ

Méndez specialises in regional food produce from the north of Spain and offers an extraordinary range which includes Cabrales cheese, lamprey and delicious Padrón peppers. It also bakes its own bread in the Galician style.

🕂 F8 ✉ Ayala 65 ☎ 402 43 78 🚇 Lista

MUSEO DEL JAMÓN

There are five branches of the Ham Museum in the city, each a spectacular testament to the fact that vegetarianism in Spain has a long way to go. *Jamón serrano* is the most popular, while *jamón de Jabugo*, at around 8,000ptas a kilo, is the crown jewels.

🕂 cII, E9 ✉ Carrera de San Jerónimo 6 ☎ 521 03 46/57 21 🚇 Sol

RICHART

Fancy chocolates, or *bombones*, are a central part of Spanish special occasions. Richart's chocolates are a little more expensive than most, but the attention to detail is exquisite.

🕂 F8 ✉ Calle Príncipe de Vergara 26 ☎ 577 46 62 🚇 Nuñez de Balboa

Wine, cheese and *chorizo*

Spanish wine is slowly acquiring an international reputation, but Spanish cheese is not, and much of it is very good. The most 'typical' is Manchego, which varies tremendously in quality, while the strongest is Cabrales, made from a mixture of sheep's and goat's milk. As well as the hams, the Spanish *chorizos* (a kind of salami) and *morcillas* (black puddings) are worth sampling for the true flavour of Spain.

BOOKSHOPS & RECORD SHOPS

Reading about Madrid

To get an insider's view of life in the Spanish capital, one could do worse than have a look at the following Madrid novels, all available in English: Benito Pérez Galdos' *Fortunata y Jacinta*, a work of Dickensian scope and depth set in 1860s Madrid; Arturo Barea's *The Forge*, a boyhood look at life before and during the Spanish Civil War; and Camilo José Cela's *The Hive* – post-Civil War Madrid through the eyes of the 1989 winner of the Nobel Prize for Literature. Cervantes's *Don Quixote* is the great Spanish Golden Age masterpiece, but it mentions Madrid only briefly. John Hooper's *The New Spaniards* is a perceptive overview of contemporary Spain by a British journalist.

BOOKSELLER'S

The best English-language bookshop in the capital, which also has a reasonable selection of imported magazines and an excellent selection of Spanish and Latin-American literature in English translation.
🕂 E6 ✉ José Abascal 48 ☎ 442 79 59 🚇 Rubén Darío

CASA DEL LIBRO

The Casa del Libro (House of the Book), of which there are several branches in the centre, claims to stock everything. It does not, but three rambling floors do manage to give the impression of comprehensiveness. There is a well-stocked foreign literature section in the Gran Vía branch.
🕂 bl, D8 ✉ Gran Vía 29 ☎ 521 21 13 🚇 Gran Vía

CUESTA DE MOYANO

Every Sunday morning from about 10:30, the book stalls lining the road up to the Retiro from Atocha open up. Many of the books are modern and no cheaper than in the bookshops, but there is a smattering of second-hand books in other languages, and the occasional gem waiting to be found. Ideal for browsing and seeking expert advice.
🕂 E10 ✉ Calle Claudio Moyano (next to Botanical Gardens) 🚇 Atocha

EL FLAMENCO VIVE

'Flamenco lives', the name proclaims, and when you are inside Alberto Martínez's new store – incredibly, the first in Spain devoted to the true flamenco *aficionado* – you are left in no doubt. As well as offering a good selection of the music, there are books on the history of flamenco and many examples of flamenco paraphernalia.
🕂 all, D9 ✉ Calle Unión 4 ☎ 547 39 17 🚇 Opera

MADRID ROCK

Madrid's biggest and best record store. Three floors dedicated to just about everything you could wish for, complete with video screens, listening booths, a good selection of imports and a concert booking service. Smaller branches in Calle Mayor and Calle San Martín.
🕂 cl, D8 ✉ Gran Vía 25 ☎ 523 26 52 🚇 Gran Vía

TURNER

The basement contains a wide variety of foreign literature, with a particular emphasis on English and French. There is a good range of English-language tourist guides, and an excellent classical music shop next door.
🕂 E8 ✉ Calle Génova 3–5 ☎ 319 28 67 🚇 Alonso Martínez

ZIGGY DOS

The best store for second-hand, hard-to-find items. There is another branch in the Rastro.
🕂 bl, D8 ✉ Cuesta de Santo Domingo 8 ☎ 559 40 84 🚇 Santo Domingo

OTHER GOOD SHOPS

ALMORAIMA
A wide range of fans, from the cheap and cheerful to those which are almost works of art. The most expensive item is made of bone and marble and costs more than 50,000ptas.

bII, D9 ⊠ Plaza Mayor 12 ☎ 365 42 89 🔲 Sol

CASA JIMÉNEZ
The *mantillas* and shawls around the shoulders of Spanish women are one of the distinguishing dress features among women of a certain age. Casa Jiménez has been doing business for more than 70 years, with a particularly fine selection in blond lace.

F9, D9 ⊠ Preciados 42 ☎ 548 05 26 🔲 Callao/Santo Domingo

CASA YUSTAS
This hat shop, founded in 1894, may have a slightly over-military feel, but it has managed to retain much of its period charm. The defiant lack of adornment and the lengthy counter, behind which four assistants stand rigidly to attention, is typical of late 19th-century *madrileño* establishments.

bII, D9 ⊠ Plaza Mayor 30 ☎ 366 58 34 🔲 Sol

DON JUAN
Benito Gómez opened Don Juan in 1995 and sells typical but authentic objects from all over Spain, aimed at a slightly more select market than normal, such as century-old *azulejo* tiles and *Rocío* perfume bottles.

al, C8 ⊠ Plaza de la Marina Española 7 ☎ 547 12 27 🔲 Opera

PALACIOS Y MUSEOS
As its name suggests, this new store specialises in products which you would otherwise have to visit museums to find, with replicas of objects from museums both in Spain and abroad, made by the same company which supplies the replicas to the museums themselves.

F8 ⊠ Calle Goya 48 ☎ 577 10 31 🔲 Velázquez

REGALOS AR
Lladró (Spanish for porcelain) is something which many visitors to Spain like to take away with them. Regalos Ar is handily central and plentifully stocked. Also sells handicrafts and Majorca pearls.

cl, D8 ⊠ Gran Via 46 ☎ 522 68 69 🔲 Callao

SESEÑA
The only shop in Madrid which specialises in capes: an old family establishment dating back to 1901, which keeps a firm eye on maintaining quality control. Clients have included Pablo Picasso, Michael Jackson and Hillary Clinton.

cII, D9 ⊠ Calle de la Cruz 23 ☎ 531 68 40 🔲 Sol

Typically Spanish buying

Madrid is the best place in Spain to buy typically Spanish products. Gift suggestions might include a cape, a *boina* or typical Spanish gentleman's cap, a *bota de vino* or leather wine container, from which the wine is poured at arm's length into the mouth, or a typical *azulejo* tile, but there is much else of interest.

BARS BY NIGHT (*CERVECERÍAS*)

Madrid by night

There are almost 4,000 places to have a drink in Madrid. It can claim to be Europe's finest city when it comes to the sheer variety of places available for talking and drinking late into the night – sometimes very late indeed. Main bar areas in the centre are the start of the Paseo de la Castellana (sophisticated), Malasaña (thoroughly unsophisticated), Santa Ana (somewhere in between), and Chueca (gay). A late-night stroll round any of these areas is sure to throw up a personal favourite.

BAGELÜS

This is not only one bar, but several. Glitzy BageLüs is Madrid's only 24-hour leisure space, and it includes a café, restaurant and record and bookshop. There are also regular live performances and cabaret.

➕ E6 ☒ Calle María de Molina 25 ☎ 561 61 00 Ⓜ Avenida de América

CERVECERÍA ALEMANA

One of the most popular bars for visitors and always bustling with smart, efficient waiters, but it closes a little early for some tastes. A good meeting-place for the Santa Ana district.

➕ cII, D9 ☒ Plaza de Santa Ana 6 ☎ 429 70 33 Ⓜ Antón Martín

FINNEGAN'S

Of the several Irish bars and clubs currently doing great business in Madrid, this unpretentious, popular location comes the closest to having the authentic feel of an Irish country pub. Fixtures and fittings are imported: the bar, for example, used to be the counter of a draper's in County Cork.

➕ E8 ☒ Plaza de las Salesas 9 ☎ 310 05 21 Ⓜ Chueca

LA COQUETTE

Very 1960s and very studenty, La Coquette remains the only Madrid bar which is dedicated exclusively to blues music.

➕ D9 ☒ Calle de las Hileras 14 Ⓜ Opera

LA ESCONDIDA

Probably the smallest bar you have ever seen, with a wide range of wines and tasty *tapas*.

➕ bIII, D9 ☒ Plaza de Puerta Cerrada 6 ☎ 308 54 13 Ⓜ La Latina

LIBERTAD 8

A very relaxed watering-hole with nightly cabaret at 11:30PM, plenty of seating and lots of cigarette smoke.

➕ dI, E8 ☒ Calle Libertad 8 ☎ 532 11 50 Ⓜ Chueca

REPORTER

Despite regular threats of closure from the council, Reporter's convivial (and laid-back) *terraza* to the rear of the bar still manages to open up each year when summer arrives. Serves meals at lunchtime.

➕ dIII, E9 ☒ Calle Fúcar 6 ☎ 429 39 22 Ⓜ Antón Martín

TORITO

This remarkable bar is popular with non-Spaniards since most of the music it plays is Spanish. Tiny and cramped, with its walls covered in bizarre montages.

➕ E8 ☒ Calle Pelayo 4 ☎ 532 77 99 Ⓜ Chueca

VIVA MADRID

Set in the Santa Ana district, the tiled *azulejo* frontage of Viva Madrid has been photographed for a thousand guide books. Nice décor, with tables upstairs.

➕ cII, D9 ☒ Calle Manuel Fernández y González 7 ☎ 429 3640 Ⓜ Antón Martín

TERRAZAS/COCKTAIL BARS

DEL DIEGO

Founded by an ex-waiter from El Chicote, and just around the corner from it, Del Diego's superb design and highly attentive bar staff have quickly made it one of the big three *coctelerías* or cocktail bars, beside El Chicote and Le Cock, both of which are two minutes away.

cl, E8 ⊠ Calle de la Reina 12 ☎ 523 31 06 Ⓜ Gran Vía

EL CHICOTE

Opened in 1931, El Chicote is the granddaddy of Madrid's *coctelerías*, and continues to be a nocturnal reference point for the rich and famous. Legend has it that the Chicote's *mojito* was Ernest Hemingway's favourite tipple. Art-deco fixtures and alcove seating make the Chicote a memorable, though not cheap, experience.

bl, ⊠ Gran Vía 12 ☎ 532 67 37 Ⓜ Gran Vía

LAS VISTILLAS

This is the *terraza* with the best night-time views. For a slightly more peaceful atmosphere, it is a good idea to descend the steps to the area below the Viaduct.

alll, C9 ⊠ Travesía de las Vistillas Ⓜ La Latina

PASEO DE LA CASTELLANA

Collectively known as the 'Costa Castellana', there are about 20 *terrazas* between Atocha and the Plaza de Lima, not all of which are open from one year to the next. They run right up the middle of the street; with the traffic whizzing by on either side, and the music booming out; they are not places for the hard-of-hearing or quietly spoken. Perhaps the best are Bavaro Beach (Paseo del Prado), Bolero (Paseo de la Castellana 33) and Boulevard (Paseo de la Castellana 37).

E9/E8/E7 ⊠ Paseo del Prado/Paseo de Recoletos/Paseo de la Castellana
Ⓜ Atocha/Banco de España

PASEO DE PINTOR ROSALES

The *terrazas* here run along the side of the Parque del Oeste. Noisy and lots of fun.

C8, C7 ⊠ Paseo de Pintor Rosales Ⓣ April–October
Ⓜ Plaza de España/Ventura Rodríguez

PLAZA DE CONDE DE BARAJAS

Just behind the Plaza Mayor, away from the traffic, without music and with a whole square to itself, this is the most peaceful of the *terrazas*. Only open in summer.

bll, D9 ⊠ Plaza de Conde de Barajas Ⓜ Sol/Opera

Terrazas

The *terraza* bars are where young *madrileños* go to show off their suntans and to drink late into the night. It is entirely logical that during the summer, with temperatures in the upper 30s, bar culture should move outside on to the pavements, which become hectic, heaving and fun. But the *terraza* is a vague concept, and can refer to just about any bar with chairs and tables outside. Depending on the weather, they open up during April and stay open until late October.

OPERA & CLASSICAL MUSIC

Zarzuela

In the words of Edmundo de Amici, writing in 1870, the *zarzuela* is 'a piece of music somewhere between comedy and melodrama, between opera and vaudeville, with prose and verse, both recited and sung, serious and light-hearted, a very Spanish and very entertaining musical form'. Among theatre audiences of a certain age, it remains as popular in Madrid as it has ever been.

AUDITORIO NACIONAL DE MÚSICA

Madrid's finest classical music venue and the only one which can claim to be on the international classical music circuit. Home to the Spanish National Orchestra, the ONE, it runs several seasons each year, the most important of which is the ONE's own season which runs from October to June.
➕ F5 ✉ Príncipe de Vergara 146 ☎ 337 01 00 🚇 Cruz del Rayo

CIRCULO DE BELLAS ARTES

This is the best forum for contemporary classical music, with its own 'in-house' ensemble, the Grupo Círculo.
➕ dII, E9 ✉ Calle Marqués de Casa Riera 2 ☎ 531 77 00/532 44 38 🚇 Banco de España

LA CORRALA

Though not a concert venue in the ordinary sense, during the summer La Corrala is used as an outdoor location for *zarzuela* performances.
➕ cIV, D10 ✉ Calle Tribulete 12 ☎ No phone: see press for details 🚇 Lavapiés

LA FÍDULA

Between September and June recitals are given by music students in this bar on most nights of the week.
➕ dIII, E9 ✉ Calle Huertas 57 ☎ 429 29 47 🚇 Antón Martín

TEATRO MONUMENTAL

It hosts other kinds of concerts as well, but it is best known as the site where classical concerts are recorded for broadcast by the Spanish Radio and Television Orchestra and Choir.
➕ cIII, E9 ✉ Calle Atocha 65 ☎ 429 81 19/12 81 🚇 Antón Martín

TEATRO PRADILLO

This is the best place in Madrid to listen to 'world music', or indeed anything off the musical beaten track. It also hosts improvisation evenings and performance art.
➕ G5 ✉ Calle Pradillo 12 ☎ 416 90 11 🚇 See press for details 🚇 Concha Espina

TEATRO REAL

The recent history of the Teatro Real has been quiet: it has been closed since 1987 for renovation. It *may* reopen in 1997, in which case it should reclaim its rightful place amongst the grandest and most beautiful of the European opera houses.
➕ aII, C9 ✉ Plaza de Isabel II 🚇 Opera

TEATRO DE LA ZARZUELA

The *raison d'être* for this beautiful 1,300-seater concert hall is the performance of *zarzuela* (see side panel). While the Teatro Real is under renovation, it is also Madrid's official opera house.
➕ dII, E9 ✉ Calle Jovellanos 4 ☎ 429 82 25/524 54 00 🚇 Banco de España

FLAMENCO, ROCK & JAZZ

AQUALUNG

Madrid's main rock venue, with a capacity for 2,000. Sited in the La Ermita leisure complex, Aqualung is as likely to host performances by visiting British and American rock bands as by Spanish. When there is no concert, it becomes a disco.

⊞ B9 ⊠ Paseo de la Ermita del Santo 40–48 ☎ 470 23 62 ⓜ Pirámides, Marqués de Vadillo

BAR CAFÉ DEL FORO

Though it hosts concerts of straight rock, the Café del Foro also has concerts of salsa, fusion, and straight cabaret as well as occasional performances by magicians and comedians. A friendly, buzzing catch-all venue.

⊞ D7 ⊠ Calle San Andrés 38 ☎ 445 37 52 ⓜ Bilbao

CAFÉ CENTRAL

In the opinion of readers of jazz magazine *Wire*, the Café Central is amongst the best jazz venues in Europe. There are performances every night at 10:30PM from mainly Spanish, but sometimes foreign, musicians.

⊞ cIII, D9 ⊠ Plaza del Ángel 10 ☎ 369 41 43 ⓜ Sevilla, Antón Martín, Sol

CAFÉ POPULART

Live music every day, taking in jazz, blues and swing in a comfortable, semi-intellectual environment.

⊞ cIII, E9 ⊠ Calle Huertas 22 ☎ 429 84 07 ⓜ Antón Martín

CANDELA

One of the finest at the 'smoky hole' end of things. Candela's clientele are mainly gypsies from the surrounding *barrio*, the music is exclusively flamenco, and the atmosphere is highly charged, particularly after two in the morning.

⊞ cIII, D9 ⊠ Calle del Olmo at corner of Calle Olivar ⓜ Antón Martín

CASA PATAS

The best-known of Madrid's flamenco *tablaos*, a little touristy but none the less enjoyable. Midnight live performances are on Thursdays, Fridays and Saturdays, more regularly throughout the *fiesta* month of May.

⊞ cIII, D9 ⊠ Calle Cañizares 10 ☎ 369 15 74/04 96 ⓜ Tirso de Molina/Antón Martín

CLAMORES JAZZ

Jazz music is still at the heart of Clamores, but it now features tango and even karaoke. Elegant surroundings.

⊞ D7 ⊠ Calle Alburquerque 14 ☎ 445 79 38 ⓜ Bilbao

REVÓLVER CLUB

This large rock club is one of the favoured venues for visiting bands with an indie slant. It also hosts flamenco performances on Monday nights.

⊞ D7 ⊠ Calle Galileo 26 ☎ 594 27 05/26 38/26 79 ⓜ Quevedo, Argüelles

More rock than flamenco

Madrid's rock venues continue to offer visitors the chance, if they are lucky, to see performers – who would be playing much larger places at home – in relatively intimate surroundings. Ticket prices are not unreasonable, but this is generally more than compensated for at the bar. Surprisingly, there are few flamenco bars.

CLUBS & DISCOS

Rave on

The limitless capacity of *madrileños* for having fun has made Madrid a disco-owner's dream. This is the undisputed European night-life capital, where the night begins and ends very late indeed and lasts as long as you can take it. There is no concept of 'exclusive club membership', which means that everyone has access to everywhere.

ARCHY

An extremely fashionable club/restaurant which has a well-known clientele, with an intimate basement disco and a post-modern venue upstairs. With three different 'micro-environments', Archy is as good for talking in as for dancing.
✚ E7 ✉ Calle Marqués de Riscal 11 ☎ 308 31 62/27 36/21 62 ⓜ Quevedo/Iglésia

EL SOL

Chaotic and a bit shabby, but lots of fun, El Sol had strong connections with the *movida* Madrid of the 1980s. A wide variety of music and central location.
✚ cl, D9 ✉ Calle Jardines 3 ☎ 532 64 90 ⓜ Sol/Gran Via

EMPIRE

Five bars and two floors: from above you look down on the people dancing. Original design, and a clientele in the 25–35-year-old age group.
✚ dl, E8 ✉ Paseo de Recoletos 16 ☎ 431 54 27 ⓜ Colón

JOY ESCLAVA

Probably as close as Madrid gets to disco heaven, Joy Esclava's central location attracts a wide clientele. Plush, though without being forbiddingly stylish.
✚ bll, D9 ✉ Calle Arenal 11 ☎ 366 54 39/32 84/37 33 ⓜ Sol/Ópera

PALACE DISCOTHEQUE

The pulling-points for the Palace are the telephones on each table, allowing you to call another table and offer a drink or a dance to someone who has caught your eye. Also has an in-house band, an increasing rarity.
✚ bll, D9 ✉ Plaza de Isabel II, 7 ☎ 541 82 30 ⓜ Opera

PALACIO DE GAVIRIA

One of Madrid's more remarkable night-time locations. An 1851 palace, with fixtures and fittings generally intact, which reopened in 1981 as a nightspot. With its grand staircase entrance and 14 halls spread over 1,300sq m, it is an experience as well as a night out.
✚ bll, D9 ✉ Calle Arenal 9 ☎ 526 60 69 ⓜ Sol

SCALA MELÍA CASTILLA

The closest Madrid comes to the Parisian Crazy Horse, offering twice-daily good old-fashioned cabaret shows with a meal.
✚ E4 ✉ Capitán Haya 43 (Edificio Meliá Castilla) ☎ 571 44 11 ⊙ Closed Aug ⓜ Cuzco/Valdeacederas

TEATRIZ

A bar/restaurant as well as a nightclub. Teatriz is a complex of avant-garde rooms designed by Philippe Starck in the late 1980s. Incredible to look at, though unless full it can feel a little cold.
✚ F8 ✉ Calle Hermosilla 15 ☎ 577 53 79/91 95 ⓜ Serrano

CINEMAS

ALPHAVILLE

Alphaville, which opened shortly after democracy came to Spain, retains the healthy habit of showing short films before the main feature, thereby providing an outlet for talent which might otherwise go unrecognised. There is a good café downstairs. Late-night showings at weekends.

✚ C8 ✉ Calle Martín de los Heros 14 ☎ 559 38 36 Ⓜ Plaza de España

FILMOTECA ESPAÑOLA

Inaugurated in 1922 as the Cine Doré, and lovingly re-created in 1989, the Filmoteca is a godsend for cinephiles in Madrid. Four original version films are shown daily in its two theatres, with tickets three times cheaper than anywhere else. Many of the films are well-known classics; others are truly obscure, but most have something to recommend them, and it is worth taking a chance. The Filmoteca produces a monthly bulletin, and there is a good bookshop as well as pleasant bar in the foyer.

✚ cIII, E9 ✉ Calle Santa Isabel 3 ☎ 369 11 25 Ⓜ Antón Martín

IDEAL MULTICINES

The Ideal has eight theatres which range in size from 10sq m to 400sq m, and is probably Madrid's most comfortable cinema, showing a mixture of art and mainstream features. Late-night showings at weekends.

✚ cIII, D9 ✉ Calle Doctor Cortezo 6 ☎ 369 25 18/03 31 Ⓜ Sol/Tirso de Molina

OPEN-AIR CINEMA

During the summer months, the esplanade beside the bullring offers open-air films across two screens, at good prices, but the site may vary from year to year. The films are normally shown in Spanish only.

✚ H7 ✉ Plaza de las Ventas Ⓜ Las Ventas

RENOIR

Of the cluster of cinemas around the bottom of Calle Martín de los Heros (just by the Plaza de España) this is the best, showing the latest art films in five theatres of differing sizes. An original touch is in the detailed information sheets which are published (in Spanish) to accompany each film. In the Plaza de España theatre there is a good cinema bookshop, open during the week only. Late-night showings at weekends. There is another, newer Renoir in Cuatro Caminos.

✚ C8 ✉ Calle Martín de los Heros 12/Calle Raimundo Fernández Villaverde 10 ☎ 559 57 60/534 00 77 Ⓜ Plaza de España/Cuatro Caminos

Original Version

While the Spanish film industry is burgeoning, the number of cinemas is also on the increase, with 60 at the last count – ten of which show exclusively original version (not dubbed) films. Most cinemas have a *día del espectador*, or audience day, which might be a Monday or a Wednesday. Tickets on these days are half the normal price. It is worth arriving well in advance for mid- and late-evening weekend showings, particularly if a film has only just opened: queues can start forming as much as an hour before projection time. Cinema information is published in full in all the daily newspapers: earliest showings (*pasos*) are generally at 4, latest at 10:30.

Other Cinemas showing original version:

Lumiére, Pasaje de Martín de los Heros 14 (☎ 559 38 36)

Bellas Artes, Calle Marqués de Casa Riera 2 (☎ 522 50 92)

Princesa, Calle Princesa 3 (☎ 559 98 72)

Rosales, Calle Quintana 22 (☎ 541 58 00)

LUXURY HOTELS

For a double room in a luxury hotel expect to pay 25,000–50,000ptas or more. Many offer special cheap weekend rates.

Paradores

Spain's network of *paradores* – sumptuous aristocratic residences converted into luxury hotels – is no longer the well-kept secret it once was. Madrid does not have its own *parador*, but anyone wishing to travel around the country should go to Calle Velázquez 18 (☎ 435 66 41) for information and reservations.

EUROBUILDING

With 421 rooms and twin towers, this is the largest hotel in Madrid, and an example of what the Madrid of the future will look like. Located at the non-touristy, business end of the city, Euro-building is a world unto itself, part of a complex with shops, clubs, cafés, a gym and sauna.

✚ F4 ✉ Calle Padre Damián 23 ☎ 345 45 00 Ⓜ Cuzco

GRAN HOTEL REINA VICTORIA

Facing the Teatro Español in the heart of the buzzing Santa Ana district, the magnificent Reina Victoria has historical connections with the bullfighting world. There are 201 rooms.

✚ d9, CII ✉ Plaza de Santa Ana 14 ☎ 531 45 00 Ⓜ Sol

MELÍA MADRID

Centrally located in a 20-floor building, the Melía was renovated in 1992. Modern and perhaps a little too functional, but extremely spacious, with gymnasium and sauna. Part of a chain of Melía hotels in Madrid.

✚ C7 ✉ Calle Princesa 27 ☎ 541 82 00 Ⓜ Ventura Rodriguez

PALACE

Of its own choice, the Palace dropped a star in 1993. It has a reputation for being a little less formal than the Ritz, with which it has long been in competition as Madrid's best central hotel. Popular with visiting celebrities.

✚ dII, E9 ✉ Plaza de las Cortes 7 ☎ 429 13 02/75 51 Ⓜ Banco de España

RITZ

Spain's first luxury hotel, the Ritz, opened in 1910. It lives up to its name: Ritz luxury at Ritz prices. Between the spring and autumn it has a delightful terrace-restaurant.

✚ dII, E9 ✉ Plaza de la Lealtad 5 ☎ 521 28 57 Ⓜ Banco de España

SANTO MAURO

Occupies the French-style former palace of the Dukes of Santo Mauro, with a wonderful patio entrance, avant-garde decoration in the rooms and a swimming-pool. The 37 rooms are all different.

✚ E7 ✉ Calle Zurbano 36 ☎ 319 69 00 Ⓜ Rubén Dario

VILLA MAGNA

With French neo-classical décor, a good restaurant (Berceo) with a pleasant terrace, the Villa Magna is favoured by visiting businessmen for its location at the start of the Castellana.

✚ E7 ✉ Paseo de la Castellana 22 ☎ 576 75 00 Ⓜ Rubén Dario

WELLINGTON

Located in the elegant *barrio Salamanca*, and the closest luxury hotel to the Retiro Park, the 300-room Wellington is also blessed with a flamenco venue, Zambra, downstairs.

✚ F8 ✉ Calle Velázquez 8 ☎ 575 44 00 Ⓜ Retiro

Mid-Range Hotels

AROSA
With a very central location, the Arosa has long been popular with visitors, particularly families. An excellent base for exploring the night-life around the centre.

✚ cl, D8 ☒ Calle de la Salud 21 ☎ 532 16 00 ⊚ Sol

ASTURIAS
With 175 rooms, and conveniently close to the Puerta del Sol, the Asturias is particularly popular with foreign visitors. From the noise point of view, it is best to ask for an inside room.

✚ cll, D9 ☒ Calle Sevilla 2 ☎ 429 66 76 ⊚ Sevilla

CARLOS V
Located right next to the Puerta del Sol, the Carlos V has 67 rooms and, if you can get a room on the 5th floor, you will get a balcony. Bright and friendly.

✚ bll, D9 ☒ Calle Maestro Vitoria 5 ☎ 531 41 00 ⊚ Sol

CONDE DUQUE
Giving on to an enclosed square, the Conde Duque is among the more peaceful of the hotels located near the city centre.

✚ D7 ☒ Plaza del Conde Valle Suchil 5 ☎ 447 70 00 ⊚ San Bernardo

EL PRADO
Within easy reach of the Prado Museum and the Santa Ana district, El Prado occupies a lovely building which was restored in 1992. Windows are double-glazed, which means a good night's sleep in the middle of a bustling *barrio*.

✚ cll, E9 ☒ Calle Prado 11 ☎ 369 02 34 , ⊚ Antón Martín/Sevilla

GALIANO RESIDENCIA
Formerly the palace of a noble family and located on a quiet street off the Castellana, the Galiano is small, but its spacious rooms and old-world feel make it one of Madrid's better-kept secrets.

✚ E8 ☒ Calle Alcalá Galiano 6 ☎ 319 20 00/522 10 13 ⊚ Colón

INGLÉS
Clean, bright and friendly, the family-owned Inglés is pleasantly located among a maze of narrow streets within easy reach of many sights.

✚ cll, D9 ☒ Calle Echegaray 8 ☎ 429 65 51 ⊚ Sevilla

MÓNACO
Until the 1950s the Monaco was a brothel. It retains much of its charm, particularly in its intimate lobby, and each of its 32 rooms, many with supremely kitsch décor, is different. A Madrid classic.

✚ cl, E8 ☒ Calle Barbieri 5 ☎ 522 46 30 ⊚ Chueca

PINTOR
The Hawaiian-inspired lobby of this hotel is probably Madrid's tackiest, but its 176 rooms are comfortable. A good location for shopping.

✚ F8 ☒ Calle Goya 79 ☎ 435 75 45 ⊚ Goya

For a double room in a mid-range hotel expect to pay 7,000–18,000ptas.

Prices
Accommodation in Spain is divided into the normal five categories, but the issue is complicated by the hostels (*hostales*) at the lower end of the scale – a good *hostal* may be more comfortable than a poor hotel. VAT of 7 per cent has to be added to the quoted price. All the places listed on the Budget Accommodation page of this guide are *hostales*.

BUDGET ACCOMMODATION

Booking

Madrid has many hotels, and finding a room should not be hard (although harder in tourist areas). Book as far in advance as possible, and call to reconfirm. If you arrive without a reservation, there is an accommodation agency called Brújula (Head Office at Calle Princesa 1, 6th floor: 559 9705/9–7) which will book rooms in hotels in Madrid and around for 250ptas. The phone line is often busy, so it is advisable to go to either the head office or one of its branches at Atocha (8AM–10PM) and Chamartín Railway Station (7AM–11:30PM) in person.

ARMESTO

A particularly friendly *hostal* located opposite the Plaza de la Cortes. The owners have made an attempt to colour-co-ordinate the rooms.

✚ dII, E9 ✉ Calle San Agustín 6 (1st floor derecha) ☎ 429 90 31 Ⓜ Antón Martín

CERVANTES

A family-owned *hostal* set in a quiet area near the Retiro and the Prado, with 17 rooms, all with bath. Do not be put off by the rickety lift.

✚ dII, E9 ✉ Calle Cervantes 34 (2nd floor) ☎ 429 27 45/429 83 65 Ⓜ Antón Martín

LA MONTAÑA

There are five *hostales* at this address, which is located in a relatively peaceful area to the east of the centre. Decent-sized, well-lit rooms.

✚ C8 ✉ Calle Juan Álvarez Mendizabal 44 (4th floor) ☎ 547 10 88 Ⓜ Ventura Rodríguez

LORENZO

Recently redecorated, the Lorenzo is distinguished principally for its soundproof windows. Not very homely, but quite stylish.

✚ cI, E8 ✉ Calle Infantas 26 (3rd floor) ☎ 521 30 57 Ⓜ Gran Vía

RETIRO/NARVÁEZ

Two *hostales* in the same building. All the rooms have showers, but not all have a toilet. Though a little way from the centre, it has good communications. The Retiro has 16 rooms, the Narváez 11.

✚ F8 ✉ Calle O'Donnell 27 (4th floor derecha and 5th floor) ☎ 576 00 37/575 01 07 Ⓜ Príncipe de Vergara

RIESCO

This *hostal* offers 27 hotel rooms at *hostal* prices. Family run, it is located just off the Plaza del Sol, and you do not get much more central than that.

✚ dII, D9 ✉ Calle Correo 2 (3rd floor) ☎ 522 26 92 Ⓜ Sol

SUD AMERICANA

Very small (only eight rooms), but the ideal location if you plan to spend a lot of time in the area around the Prado. All rooms have showers, not all have a bath, and there are pleasant views. The slightly less appealing Hostal Coruña is in the same building.

✚ dIII, E9 ✉ Paseo del Prado 12 (6th floor) ☎ 429 25 64 Ⓜ Antón Martín/Atocha

PAZ

On a quiet street, the Paz has some rooms which overlook a courtyard with trees. Very clean, efficient and friendly.

✚ bII, D9 ✉ Calle Flora 4 (1st floor) ☎ 547 30 47 Ⓜ Sol/Opera

MADRID
travel facts

ARRIVING & DEPARTING

Before you go
- Visitors from Schengen Treaty countries (Belgium, France, Germany, Luxembourg, the Netherlands and Portugal) do not need a passport, and have the same rights as in their own country. Visitors to Spain from Britain require a valid passport in the absence of a British ID card.
- Visas are not required for US, Canadian, New Zealand, UK, Eire or other EU nationals for stays of under 90 days. Australian nationals visiting Spain do require a visa. Ask the nearest Spanish Consulate for information.
- Vaccinations are not required unless you are coming from a known infected area.

When to go
- April to early July and mid-September to mid-November are the best periods.
- July and August are very hot.
- The quietest months are January and February, but it can be cold.

Climate
- Winter lasts from early December until the end of February.
- March can be damp and unpleasant.
- Summers are hot and dry: any rain is unusual between June and October.
- Spring and autumn are generally lovely: little rain, blue skies and a pleasant temperature.

Arriving by air
- All flights arrive at Barajas Airport. The Spanish national airline is Iberia.
- Barajas Information ☎ 393 60 00
  Iberia Information
  ☎ 587 87 87/ 47 47

Infoiberia ☎ 329 56 67
Flight Information
☎ 305 83 43/ 44/45.
- A bus leaves Barajas every 15 minutes from 5AM to midnight (look for EMT signs). It arrives at an area directly beneath the Plaza de Colón. To get from here to the Colón metro, you have to go up to street level and cross the square, a five-minute walk. There is no train connection with the airport. A taxi from the airport to the city centre should take around 20 minutes.

Arriving by train
- Trains from France, Portugal and Northern Spain arrive at Chamartín Station.
- Trains from southern and eastern Spain and express services from Lisbon arrive at Atocha Station. Both are on the metro system.
- Between Chamartín and Atocha are two other stations, Recoletos and Nuevos Ministerios, where you can get off, but not board, trains.

Arriving by car
- Two ring roads circle Madrid: an outer one (M40) and an inner (M30). Head for Paseo de la Castellana: this is central Madrid's main artery and most central locations are easily reached from here.

Arriving by bus
- There are many private bus companies in Spain. Many pass through the Estación Sur de Autobuses on Calle Canarias, which is near the Palos de la Frontera metro station.

Customs regulations
- EU residents do not have to declare goods imported for personal use.
- Visitors can carry up to 1 million ptas in cash.

Essential Facts

Travel insurance

- EU nationals are entitled to health care under EU law, if they have an E111 form, but it is safer (and quicker) to take out full health and travel insurance before leaving. Non-EU residents should take out private medical and travel insurance before leaving.

Opening hours

- Shops: 9–1:30, 5–8
- Department stores: 9–9
- Churches: 9:30–1:30, 5–7:30
- Museums: considerable variation, but many close on Mondays
- Banks: Mon–Fri 9–2; between October and May many banks open from 9–1 on Saturdays.

Public holidays

- 1 Jan; 6 Jan; Good Friday; Easter Monday; 1 May; 2 May; 15 May; 15 Aug; 12 Oct; 1 Nov; 9 Nov; 6 Dec; 8 Dec; 25 Dec.

Money matters

- The Spanish currency is the peseta, abbreviated to pta.
- Notes: 1,000ptas, 2,000ptas, 5,000ptas, 10,000ptas.
- Coins: 1pta, 5 ptas (old style: silver; new style: small bronze), known informally as duros; 10ptas (rare); 25ptas (old style: silver; new style: small bronze, with hole); 50, 100 , 200 and 500ptas. Since January 1997, old-style coins are no longer legal tender.
- Most major travellers' cheques can be changed at banks. American Express offers best travellers' cheque rates.
- Credit cards are now accepted in all large establishments and an increasing number of smaller ones.
- There are many clearly indicated (multi-lingual) cash points: ServiRed and TeleBanco take all major credit cards.

Etiquette

- Though they do not normally form orderly queues, Spaniards are generally aware of their place in the service order.
- Though there are clearly marked 'No Smoking' areas in many restaurants, many Spaniards smoke. Smoking on public transport is banned.
- Stretching and yawning in public is considered vulgar.
- Do not be worried about using your voice to attract attention in bars and restaurants (say 'Oiga'). You may be ignored if you do not.
- In restaurants, it can take longer to get the bill than the meal.
- Drinks are normally paid for before you leave the bar, not on a round by round basis.
- Tipping is discretionary, but around 10 per cent is normal.

Women or lone travellers

- Spain is a safe country in which to travel, but the normal common-sense rules apply.
- Avoid poorly lit areas and the parks after dark.
- Women, particularly blondes, may be wolf-whistled.

Places of worship

- Dress formally: do not wear shorts.
- Do not enter during Mass.
- Flash photography is not normally permitted.

Student travellers

- Viajes TIVE Calle Fernando el Católico 88 (☎ 543 02 08 🅼 Moncloa) organised by the Comunidad de Madrid, offers many student travel discounts, travel cards and insurance.

Time differences
- Spanish time is one hour ahead of GMT.

Toilets
- Public toilets barely exist, and hygiene in bars and smaller restaurants is not always at a premium, though there is generally paper available. Some bars keep the key behind the bar.

Electricity
- The standard current is 220 volts.
- Plugs are of the 'round' two-pin type.
- Travel plugs can be found at Corte Inglés department stores.

Tourist Offices in Madrid
- For information about the city: Municipal Tourist Office, Plaza Mayor 3 ☎ 366 54 77/588 16 36 ◑ Mon–Fri 10–8; Sat 10–2.
- For information about the area surrounding Madrid: Regional Tourist Offices: Calle Princesa 1 (Torre de Madrid) ☎ 902 100 007/541 23 25/901 300 600 ◑ Mon–Fri 9–7, Sat 9:30–1; Calle Duque Medinaceli 2 ☎ 429 49 51 ◑ Mon–Fri 9–7, Sat 9–1.
- Tourist information is also available at Barajas Airport and Chamartín Station.

Spanish National Tourist Offices Overseas
- UK: 57–58 St James's Street, London SW1A 1LD (☎ 0171 499 0901)
- Canada: 2 Bloor Street West, 34th Floor, Toronto, Ontario, M4W 3EZ (☎ 416 961 31 31)
- USA:
  8383 Wilshire Blvd, Suite 960, Beverly Hills, Los Angeles, Cal 90211 (☎ 1213 658 71 88/71 92)
  666 5th Ave, New York, NY 10103 (☎ 212 265 88 22)

PUBLIC TRANSPORT

How to use the metro
- Station entrances are indicated by name and symbol.
- Passes are available for one month's travel. These also entitle you to travel on buses.
- Metro services run from 6:30AM until 1:30AM.

How to use the bus
- Routes run from 6AM–midnight daily, about every 15 minutes. All night buses (midnight–6AM) start in the Plaza de la Cibeles, but are less regular (every 30 minutes between midnight and 3AM; every hour after that).
- Flag the bus down if it does not look like stopping.
- Pay the driver or stamp your pass in the machine next to the driver's seat.
- To request a stop, press the hard-to-spot red button.

Where to get maps
- Metro maps are (theoretically) available from the ticket counter.
- Travel maps can be bought at newspaper stands (*kioskos*).
- Metro platforms have detailed local street maps indicating which exit is suitable for you.

Types of ticket
- For the metro: *sencillo* (single journey). and *billete de diez* (10-journey pass) can be bought from newspaper stands and tobacconists; *bono mensual* (monthly pass) entitles you to travel on both the metro and buses, and is available over the counter, with a photograph and identification.

Taxis
- These are cheap enough to make a reasonable travel alternative,

particularly if you are a group of four. There are taxi-ranks in key locations, but normally you will have to hail a taxi.

- There is a charge for boarding, and a charge for every km travelled at more than 20km per hour. A supplement is also levied after midnight, and on Sundays and public holidays. Journeys to the airport incur an airport supplement.
- Take only taxis with a green light on top. Check that the driver has reset the taximeter before you set off, particularly if you are at a taxi-rank.

MEDIA & COMMUNICATIONS

Telephones

- Public telephones take 5pta, 25pta and 100pta coins. There is a minimum charge for an inner-city call. Phone cards are available from newspaper stands, though most phones do not yet accept credit cards.
- Most bars have telephones; if not a pay-phone, you are charged according to the number of units used.
- Telefónica (the Spanish phone company) have a huge public call office on Gran Vía 30 (Mon–Sat 9AM–midnight; Sun and public hols noon–midnight). You queue up for a cabin number, then pay afterwards at the central counter. Other public phones are at the Palacio de Comunicaciones in Cibeles (Mon–Sat 8AM–midnight, Sun and public hols 8AM–10PM); and Paseo de Recoletos 41 (Mon–Fri 9AM–midnight; Sat, Sun and public hols noon–midnight).
- Cheap rate for calls is 10PM to 8AM daily.

Sending a letter or postcard

- Buy stamps from post offices (few and far between) or tobacconists. Tobacconists are indicated by a yellow and green 'T' sign on the wall.
- Madrid's most central post office is in Plaza de la Cibeles, a huge building with many counters and long queues.
- Post boxes are yellow with two slots, one marked 'Madrid' and the other for everywhere else (marked *Provincias y extranjero*).

Newspapers and magazines

- The most important daily papers are *El País* (left of centre); *El Mundo* (centre); *Diario 16* (centre) and *ABC* (right of centre). The sports paper *Marca* is Spain's best-selling newspaper on a Monday. Good weekly news magazines are *Tiempo* and *Epoca*, while *El Mundo's* city guide, *Metropoli*, is published every Friday and is the best of the available ones. There is also the weekly *Guía del Ocio* (Leisure Guide). *Lookout* is an English-language monthly directed at English-speaking residents in Spain.

Radio and television

- There are five non-paying TV stations in Madrid: TVE 1 and TVE 2 (state-run), TeleMadrid (local), Antena 3 (populist, biased) and Tele 5 (Silvio Berlusconi). The pay channel Canal + is good for films, sport and quality documentaries: like TVE 2, it shows original version films.
- There are four national radio stations catering for different tastes.

International newsagents

- Foreign newspapers are normally available from lunchtime on day of publication, and at about twice the home price, from *kioskos*. The *kioskos* at the western end of Puerta del Sol (24 hours), in Puerta de Alcalá, and in Plaza de la Cibeles are reliable, with a range of foreign magazines. FNAC (Calle Preciados) and the various VIPS stores also stock foreign press.

EMERGENCIES

Sensible precautions

- Carry valuables in a belt, pouch or similar – not in a pocket.
- Do not wear bags over one shoulder.
- Do not keep valuables in front section of rucksack. If possible, wear rucksack on your front whilst on public transport.
- Be aware of street tricks around tourist attractions: these include distracting you in conversation, or spraying foam on your back and then offering to clean it off, while someone else grabs your bag.
- Avoid parks at night. The *barrio popular* (south of the Puerta del Sol) has a high crime rate.
- Try to look as though you know where you are going.

Lost property

- Municipal Lost Property Office: Plaza Legazpi 7 ☎ 588 43 46/44 🚇 Metro Legazpi 🕐 Mon–Fri 9–2.
- For objects lost on the metro, try Cuatro Caminos station ☎ 522 49 00.
- For objects lost on a bus, EMT, Calle Alcántara 24–26 ☎ 401 31 00 🚇 Metro Lista. Ask for *objetos perdidos*.

- For objects lost on non-metro trains, call the relevant station and ask for *objetos perdidos*.
- A lost passport should be reported to your Embassy.
- If you wish to claim insurance on a loss, you have to file the loss with a *comisaría* or police station.

Medicines

- Chemist is *farmacia* in Spanish and is normally indicated by a flashing green cross; open 9:30–2 and 5–8. Outside these hours, there is a rota of *farmacias de guardia* (all-night chemists), and outside opening hours there is a list of these in the window, with the closest ones highlighted. These are also listed in the daily papers.
- Madrid's chemists are often quite happy to let you have prescription medicines without a prescription.

Emergency telephone numbers

Police (Local) ☎ 092
Police (National) ☎ 091
Police (Guardia Civil) ☎ 062 or 533 11 00
Ambulance ☎ 588 44 00/45 00/46 00
Red Cross Ambulance ☎ 522 22 22
English Language Helpline ☎ 559 13 93
Telephone Information (Spain) ☎ 003
Telephone Information (International) ☎ 025.

Embassies and consulates

Australian Embassy ☎ 570 02 53/579 04 28
British Embassy ☎ 319 02 08/319 02 00
Canadian Embassy ☎ 431 43 00
German Embassy ☎ 319 91 00
French Embassy ☎ 435 55 60

Irish Embassy ☎ 576 35 00
Italian Embassy
☎ 577 65 38/577 65 29
United States Embassy
☎ 577 40 00.

LANGUAGE

- The level of English does not generally exceed 'OK'. Explain clearly, repeatedly and with hand signals. Spanish is phonetic, so once you have mastered a few basic rules, you should be understood.

Pronunciation

c before an e or an i, and z are like th in thin
c in other cases is like c in cat
g before an e or an i, and j are a guttural sound which does not exist in English – rather like the ch in loch
g in other cases is like g in get
h is normally silent
ll is similar to y
y is like the i in onion

- Use the formal third person 'usted' when speaking to strangers; the informal 'tu' is used when speaking to friends or younger people.

Courtesies

good morning buenos días
good afternoon/evening buenos tardes
good night buenas noches
hello (informal) hola
goodbye (informal) hasta luego/hasta pronto
hello (answering the phone) ¿Diga?
goodbye adios
please por favor
thank you gracias
you're welcome de nada
how are you? (formal) ¿como está?
how are you? (informal) ¿que tal?
I'm fine estoy bien
I'm sorry lo siento

excuse me (in a bar) oiga
excuse me (in a crowd) lo siento

Basic vocabulary

yes/no sí/no
I do not understand no entiendo
I am not from here no soy de aquí
left/right izquierda/derecha
entrance/exit entrada/salida
open/closed abierto/cerrado
good/bad bueno/malo
big/small grande/pequeño
with/without con/sin
more/less más/menos
near/far cerca/lejos
hot/cold caliente/frío
early/late temprano/tarde
here/there aquí/allí
now/later ahora/más tarde
today/tomorrow hoy/mañana
yesterday ayer
how much is it? ¿cuánto es?
when? ¿cuándo?
where is the...? ¿dónde está...?
do you have...? ¿tiene...?

INDEX

INDEX

CityPack
Madrid

Written by Jonathan Holland
Edited, designed and produced by
[AA] Publishing

Maps © The Automobile Association 1997
Fold-out map © RV Reise- und Verkehrsverlag Munich · Stuttgart
© Cartography: GeoData

Distributed in the United Kingdom by AA Publishing, Norfolk House, Priestley Road, Basingstoke, Hampshire, RG24 9NY.

The contents of this publication are believed correct at the time of printing. Nevertheless, the publishers cannot be held responsible for any errors or omissions or for changes in the details given in this guide or for the consequences of any reliance on the information provided by the same. Assessments of attractions, hotels, restaurants and so forth are based upon the author's own personal experience and, therefore, descriptions given in this guide necessarily contain an element of subjective opinion which may not reflect the publishers' opinion or dictate a reader's own experiences on another occasion.
We have tried to ensure accuracy in this guide, but things do change and we would be grateful if readers would advise us of any inaccuracies they may encounter.

A CIP catalogue record for this book is available from the British Library.

ISBN 0 7495 1427 2

Published by AA Publishing (a trading name of Automobile Association Developments Limited, whose registered office is Norfolk House, Priestley Road, Basingstoke, Hampshire RG24 9NY. Registered number 1878835).

Colour separation by Daylight Colour Art Pte Ltd, Singapore
Printed and bound by Dai Nippon Printing Co (Hong Kong) Ltd.

Acknowledgements
The Automobile Association wishes to thank the following libraries and museums for their assistance in the preparation of this book: Bridgeman Art Library, London 37b. *King Henry VIII* by Hans Holbein the Younger, Thyssen-Bornemisza; 41 *The Naked Maja* by Francisco de Goya y Lucientes, The Prado; 47a. *The Adoration of the Magi* by El Greco, Museo Lazaro Galdiano. Mary Evans Picture Library 12. Museo Cerralbo, Madrid 27. Museo de America, Madrid 26b. Spectrum Colour Library 8, 52. The remaining photographs are held in the Association's own library (AA Photo Library) and were taken by Rick Strange with the exception of pages 7, 29, 36, 38a, 43a, 43b, 50, 51 which were taken by Jerry Edmanson, pages 20, 21 taken by Philip Enticknap and pages 18, 55, 58 taken by Tony Oliver.

Cover photographs
Main picture: Spectrum Colour Library. Inset top: Pictures Colour Library.
Inset bottom: AA Photo Library (R. Strange)

JOINT SERIES EDITORS *Josephine Perry and Rebecca Snelling*
COPY EDITOR *Caroline Chapman* VERIFIER *Mona King* INDEXER: *Marie Lorimer*

Titles in the CityPack series
- Amsterdam ● Atlanta ● Bangkok ● Barcelona ● Berlin ● Boston ●
- Brussels & Bruges ● Chicago ● Florence ● Hong Kong ● Istanbul ● Lisbon ●
- London ● Los Angeles ● Madrid ● Miami ● Montréal ● Moscow ● Munich ●
- New York ● Paris ● Prague ● Rome ● San Francisco ● Singapore ● Sydney ●
- Tokyo ● Toronto ● Venice ● Vienna ● Washington, D.C. ●